The Christian Family Bedtime Reading Book

EDITED BY

Ron & Lyn Klug

Augsburg Publishing House

Minneapolis

The
Christian Family
Bedtime
Reading
Book

Copyright © 1982 Augsburg Publishing House

Library of Congress Catalog Card No. 82-70952

International Standard Book No. 0-8066-1927-9

Designed and illustrated by Koechel/Peterson Design, Minneapolis, Minnesota.

Manufactured in the United States of America

Contents

Introduction .7

Stories and Poems

Bedtime Wishes 9
by M. Ogden
After wishing to be various animals,
Tim decides he's happy to be a little boy.

Nighttime .10
A poem by Mabel N. McCaw

Lullaby Story 11
A poem by Carol Greene

Sid's Spooky Closet 13
by Eileen Cole
Sid is afraid of monsters in the closet
until he confronts them.

Shadows .14
A poem by Esther A. Middlewood

Michael's Problem 14
by Betty M. Hockett
Michael feels bad at bedtime
until he asks for forgiveness.

Good Night 17
A poem by Victor Hugo

Anything—Even Socks 17
by Joyce K. Ellis
Denny learns he can pray about
anything—even lost socks.

Teddy's Friend 19
by Mildred Sallee
When a new boy with a broken leg moves into
the neighborhood, Teddy makes a friend.

The Birthday Party 21
by Helen Kronberg
Mary reluctantly invites Ramon to her birthday
party, but he turns out to be a good guest.

Friday Helpers 23
by Ann Hudson Downs
Brad and David have nothing to do until they
get the paper and mail for elderly Mrs. Brown.

Kitten Fight 25
by Catharine Brandt
Danny and Angie struggle
over the ownership of a kitten.

The Scary Scritch 28
by Peg Roberts
David is afraid of a noise outside his window
until he discovers it is his cat, Marmalade.

Under the Bed 30
A poem by Eileen Cole

Night Sounds 30
A poem by Betty Brown

Michael's Mitten 31
by Donna Bobb
When Michael's mitten is lost, he learns
about caring for God's creatures.

Everything, Praise the Lord! 32
A poem adapted from Psalm 148
by Carol Greene

Roller Skates 33
by Mae M. Vanderboom
Even on her birthday, Jean shares her new
roller skates with her friend.

Grandmother's Little Game 35
by Claire Lynn
Grandma teaches Karen the secret of happiness.

The Circus Balloon 37
by Penny Jans
Jamie chooses a helium balloon and learns
we don't always make right choices.

Jenny's Droopy Tulip 39
by Martha P. Johnson
When Jenny's class performs at a nursing home,
her mistake helps everyone relax.

When Will the Sun Shine? 42
by Sharon Ihnen
After five rainy days, Andy is happy
to see the sun, but he still values the rain.

When God Made the World 44
An action poem by Elizabeth Friedrich

A Problem for Robby 45
by Lois Kaufmann
*Robby learns to appreciate
his handicapped father.*

What's the Difference? 48
by Lois Holm
*Kathy is afraid she looks funny, but she talks
with other children and learns they all think
they have something wrong with them too.*

Tassy, Come Home 50
by Sue Richterkessing
*When her kitten is lost in a storm,
Mary Elizabeth prays and the cat is found.*

Every Dog Should Have a Boy 52
by Betty Lou Mell
*Although Jerry can't have a dog of his own,
he makes friends with a neighbor's dog.*

The Boy Who Loved the Wind 54
by Betty Lou Mell
*Johnny prays that God will
send the wind again.*

**Mr. Grumble and
the Missing Smile** 57
by Gloria A. Truitt
*Mr. Grumble is a grouchy neighbor until
the children help him find his lost cat.*

Carlos Sees God's Fireworks 60
by Elizabeth Friedrich
*Carlos overcomes his fear
of lightning and thunder.*

A Good Feeling 61
by Verna Sherman
*Karla is upset by the coming of a new teacher,
but learns to "trust and do good."*

Stolen Treasure 62
by Lois Kaufmann
*Billy falsely accuses a friend of stealing,
then asks for forgiveness.*

Move Along 65
by Ron Matthies
*Craig is upset about moving
until he makes new friends.*

The Broken Window 68
by Elizabeth Wedge
*At bedtime, David learns
to ask for forgiveness.*

God Is Always Near 71
A poem by Mabel N. McCaw

Love One Another 71
by Helen Kronberg
*Jane has trouble with a boy at school
until she helps him learn to read.*

The Boy Who Liked God 73
by Ron Matthies
*When Billy accidentally kills a bird,
he learns that God forgives.*

David and the Jellyfish 76
by Sue Guist
*When David helps his brother Billy overcome
his fear of the dark, he also overcomes his fear
of the water.*

Good-Night, Dear World 79
A poem by Solveig Paulson Russell

A Nickel Bet 79
by Craig Nagel
Robin learns some important things about God.

Joey's Surprise 81
by Ann Hudson Downs
*Joey is sick on his birthday, but his teacher
and friends come to sing outside his window.*

Billy's Promise 83
by Kit Lambeth
*Billy takes a visually handicapped
girl to a farm.*

Autumn Sigh 86
by Craig Nagel
*Timmy dislikes autumn until he learns about
the cycles of birth and death, going away
and returning.*

One of Those Days 88
by Ron Matthies
*George Henry has a bad day but learns that
we sometimes get angry at those we love most.*

When Wendy Came 91
by Craig Nagel
Robin learns to appreciate the new baby.

Friends Again 94
by Susan Davis Sandberg
*When Glen and Rick are fighting at bedtime,
their father punishes the wrong one,
then asks forgiveness.*

Mean Herbie 97
by Gloria A. Truitt
*Johnny lends his skates and makes
a friend of ''mean'' Herbie.*

Love Is a Helper 99
by Ann Hudson Downs
*When their mother has to be away,
Julie and Johnny learn to help.*

Jerry's Train Ride 102
by Ann L. Lamp
*On Jerry's first train ride, he learns that
God watches over him wherever he goes.*

The Why Boy 104
by James S. Kerr
*Jimmy asks a lot of questions, and sometimes
he gets some interesting answers.*

I Am Glad 107
A poem by Ruth Cox Anderson

Prayers

**Jesus, Tender Shepherd,
Hear Me** 109
by Mary L. Duncan

A Children's Prayer 109
by Gloria A. Truitt

Dear Father, Hear and Bless 110
Author unknown

Both Strong and Gentle 110
by Lois Walfrid Johnson

Moon and Stars 110
by Ron and Lyn Klug

We're Thankful, Lord 111
by Ron and Lyn Klug

People Who Take Care of Me 111
by Lois Walfrid Johnson

The Moon and Planet Earth 111
by Chris Jones

Thank You, God 112
by Lois Walfrid Johnson

At Day's End 112
by Lois Walfrid Johnson

People Who Work at Night 113
by Ron and Lyn Klug

My Family 113
by Lois Walfrid Johnson

Nights Are for Resting 113
by Ron and Lyn Klug

The Dark Is Friendly 114
by Chris Jones

Thunder and Lightning 114
by Lois Walfrid Johnson

Messed Up Days 114
by Chris Jones

Lullabies

God My Father, Loving Me 115

The Quiet Nighttime 116

**He's Got the Whole World
in His Hands** 117

Hush, Little Baby 118

Kumbaya .119

**All Praise to Thee,
My God, This Night** 120

**Father, We Thank Thee
for the Night** 121

Who Made the Stars 121

Jesus Loves Me When I'm Sad 122

Jesus Loves Me, Jesus Loves Me . . 122

All Through the Night 123

We Thank Thee, Lord 124

Acknowledgments 125

Introduction

Bedtime can be the best of times or the worst of times for the family, a time of conflict or a time of warm sharing. One of the best ways to make bedtime a positive experience is to plan a bedtime ritual that includes reading aloud, singing, and praying.

"Few activities create a warmer relationship between child and grownup than reading aloud," says Nancy Larrick, author of *A Parent's Guide to Children's Reading*. "It is deeply flattering to be read to and have the undivided attention of an adult. And for the adult, there is great satisfaction in sharing a child's absorption in words and pictures."

Because we felt the need for a bedtime reading book for the Christian family, we have gathered this collection of stories, poems, prayers, and lullabies.

Some of the stories in this book and many of the poems, prayers, and lullabies are written to help children overcome that natural fear of the dark and their anxiety about storms or "monsters" in the closet and under the bed. Some stories deal with common childhood experiences—friendship, sickness, moving, having a new teacher, losing a pet, welcoming a new baby into the family, and having "nothing to do." All the stories communicate Christian values such as love, trust, forgiveness, self-acceptance, sympathy, and caring. Without preaching or lecturing, we can teach these values to our children by means of the stories. Dr. Fitzhugh Dodson, author of *How to Parent*, said, "Books can have a tremendous influence on a preschool child. When you read him a book, what goes in one ear does not come out the other."

The poems and prayers in the book also encourage children to have a positive view of nighttime and an appreciation of moon and stars and wind.

We have also included a section of lullabies. Parents and children can learn together these gentle songs which reassure children of God's forgiveness and love and care. Although the lullabies are meant to be sung, the words can also be read as poems.

Some of the stories in this book and many of the poems, prayers, and lullabies can be used with preschoolers. Others are more appropriate for children in the early elementary grades. By second or third grade many children will be able to read these stories for themselves. But don't, for that reason, stop reading to them. They will still enjoy the warm relationship that is created when a book is shared.

As you use this book, you probably will develop your own bedtime ritual. Perhaps it could include a few stories, a poem or two, then one or more lullabies, and a closing prayer. Our prayer is that both you and your children will be blessed by this time together in God's presence.

Bedtime Wishes

M. Ogden

"Come on, Tim," said his mother. "It's time to take a bath and get ready for bed."

Tim's mother filled the big white tub with steamy water and bubbles, then handed Tim a washcloth. "In you go!" she said.

"Oh, phooey!" said Tim. "I wish I was a whale. Then I wouldn't have to take a bath."

"Yes, you would," said his mother. "Only you would bathe in cold, salty sea-water instead of in a nice, warm tub."

"I wouldn't like that!" said Tim. "So I wish I was a giraffe. Then I wouldn't have to wash!"

"Oh, yes, you would," said his mother. "And you would have to wash a big, long neck instead of your little, short one!" And she washed Tim's neck.

"Well, that wouldn't be much fun!" said Tim. "So I wish I was an octopus. Then I wouldn't have to wash!"

"Oh, yes, you would," said his mother. "But you would have eight elbows and arms instead of only two." And she washed Tim's elbows and arms.

"I wouldn't like that!" said Tim. "So I wish I was a giant two-headed monster! Then I would never wash!"

"Oh, yes, you would. Only you would have to wash two giant faces instead of one small one!" said Tim's mother. And she washed Tim's face.

Soon it was time for Tim to hop out of his bath. He dried off on a big, soft towel. He was all clean.

"Don't forget to brush your teeth," called his mother.

When Tim was all done, he climbed into his bed. His mother came in to say good-night.

"Good-night!" said Tim. "But I don't want to go to sleep. I wish I was an owl. Then I could stay up all night."

"Yes, you could," said his mother. "But would you really want to stay out all night in a drafty, old tree instead of in a warm, snuggly bed? And would you like to sleep all day while the sun is shining and there are so many nice things to do?"

"No!" said Tim. "I wouldn't like that at all." And he snuggled down in his warm, clean bed and closed his eyes. Suddenly Tim sat straight up in bed. "I'm glad to be a little boy after all," he said, "and I want to say 'thank you' to God."

Tim and his mother knelt beside the bed while Tim prayed. "Thank you, God, for making me a little boy. And thank you for my home and family."

When Tim crawled back into bed, he pulled the cover under his chin. Before he knew it, he was fast asleep.

Nighttime

Mabel N. McCaw

The jolly sun tells us good-night
when end of day draws nigh
by splashing orange, red, and gold
across the western sky.

And then the night comes quietly
to tuck the sky in bed
and hang the starry lantern lights
to keep watch overhead.

Lullaby Story

Carol Greene

Come to bed now, Blinky.
Close your sleepy eyes.
And dream of fuzzy panda bears
all snuggled in their panda lairs.
My Blinky, come to bed.

Come to bed now, Blinky.
Close your sleepy eyes.
And dream of drowsy porcupines
all tangled in each other's spines.
My Blinky, come to bed.

Come to bed now, Blinky.
Close your sleepy eyes.
And dream of dozing bumblebees
all snoring in their hollow trees.
My Blinky, come to bed.

Come to bed now, Blinky.
Close your sleepy eyes.
And dream of baby kangaroos
all pouched in mamas for a snooze.
My Blinky, come to bed.

Come to bed now, Blinky.
Close your sleepy eyes.
And dream of children everywhere
all safe in Jesus' loving care.
My Blinky, come to bed.

Sid's Spooky Closet

Eileen Cole

Every night, before Sid turned out his light, he closed his closet door tightly— very tightly.

One night Aunt Mary saw him doing this.

"Why do you close that door so tightly?" she asked.

"Because," said Sid, "there are monsters in the closet."

Aunt Mary smiled. "Really?" she asked. She looked in the closet. "I don't see any monsters."

Sid could feel himself blushing. "Not right now," he said. "Only when it's dark. If the door is open, I think I see monster faces, and my clothes seem to move."

"I see," said Aunt Mary thoughtfully. "You mean, as soon as the light goes out, monsters just pop into your closet, out of nowhere, and put your clothes on?"

She was asking kindly, but Sid didn't feel like answering at first. He could still feel his face burning.

"Oh," he sighed at last, "I know it's not really true. I know it's silly, but I'm still afraid. I don't know what to do about it."

"There's only one thing to do about a fear that you know is silly," said Aunt Mary.

"What's that?" asked Sid.

"Confront it," she said. "Face up to it. Well, good-night, Sid." And she kissed his cheek, turned out the light, and left the room.

For a few minutes, Sid lay quietly, getting used to the dark and thinking about what his aunt had said. He glanced at the closed closet door.

"Face up to it?" he whispered to himself. "Confront it?"

Then Sid knew what that meant. He knew what he had to do, although the thought made his hair stand on end.

Slowly he sat up in bed. He threw back the covers, clenched his teeth, and walked right up to the closet. He put his hand on the cold knob. Then he stopped. He thought he heard something moving inside.

"Nonsense!" Sid snapped out loud, and he pulled the door open.

Nothing ate him. Nothing growled. Nothing even moved, except his knees which were shaking a little.

Now Sid felt braver. He walked into the closet. He felt his boots and a football with his foot. A shirt brushed against his face. He waved his arms and felt all around the closet.

No monsters.

Sid started laughing. Suddenly he felt so good, so proud, so relieved!

Still laughing, he climbed back into bed and was soon asleep. He didn't even notice whether he had closed the closet door or left it open.

Shadows

Esther A. Middlewood

The moon shines through the window.
It makes the shadows tall.
They move and dance and run along
the ceiling and the wall.

I'm not afraid, I tell myself,
of shadows in the night.
For I can chase them all away
by turning on my light.

Michael's Problem

Betty M. Hockett

"Dinner is ready!" called Mother.

"I—I guess I don't want any dinner tonight," answered Michael in a funny-sounding voice from the rocking chair in the living room.

Mother quickly appeared in the kitchen door. "What? No dinner? Are you sick?"

Michael squeezed down a little tighter in the chair. "No! I'm OK! Just not hungry!"

"If you're not sick, I think you had better come and eat a little bit anyway," Mother said. "We're having your favorite fruit salad with whipped cream and nuts. I know you never turn that down!"

Michael sighed and obeyed his mother. "But I know I won't want to eat," he said.

All the members of the family were in a happy mood during the meal. That is, everyone except Michael.

Mother looked at him anxiously. "You aren't even eating the fruit salad, Michael. Do you have a fever?" She reached over to feel his forehead. "No, you feel cool enough. What's the problem?"

With his eyes looking down at his plate, Michael mumbled a bit crossly, "I'm all right."

Janie, Michael's older sister, continued the conversation in a cheery voice. "You know, in our class we've been talking about laws. We're supposed to be watching for people who break the laws, you know, like jaywalking and not putting money in the parking meters and things like that. We've talked about other ways that people cheat too. We're learning that laws are for our good."

Suddenly Michael looked at Janie with a frown. "Can I be excused?" he asked gruffly.

Mother glanced at Michael, looking puzzled. "Yes, I guess so. You're not eating anyway."

Michael hurried back into the living room. Without bothering to turn on the light, he plopped down into the rocking chair. He hugged his knees up tight under his chin.

"Janie talks too much," he muttered under his breath. "I don't like her talk about cheaters and people who break laws. Nobody's perfect!"

For quite a while Michael sat all by himself, feeling worse by the minute. Earlier than usual, he went off to bed. He closed his bedroom door tightly and turned on the light by his bed. The brightness caused a small plaque on his desk to glow. The words *Jesus Loves Me* stood out clearly.

Michael turned his back on the desk. "I'd rather be in the dark. Besides, I doubt if Jesus loves me tonight." Off went the light as soon as possible.

"Michael," said Mother quietly as she opened the door a bit. "May I come in?"

Down inside Michael thought, I wish she wouldn't, but out loud he said, "I guess so."

"I wanted to pray with you before you went to sleep. We always do that, you know."

"I know. But I guess maybe tonight I won't."

"I'm thinking, Michael, that you must have a problem. May I help with it?" Mother patted his arm lovingly.

"It'll be OK tomorrow."

"The Bible says that we can talk to God about all of our problems."

"But I don't think God will want to listen to me tonight," said Michael.

"He is always ready to listen and to help us," his mother reminded.

Michael thought a moment and then asked, "Even when we've done something bad?"

"Even when we've done something bad. And the longer we put off talking to God about it, the worse we feel."

Suddenly Michael's eyes filled with big tears that spilled out onto his cheeks and chin. "I don't want to feel bad any longer. I've felt bad all day today, ever since our social studies test."

"Let's talk to God about it, shall we?"

Michael nodded tearfully. He sat up in bed and leaned his head against his mother's arm. He prayed, "Dear God, I didn't mean to cheat in the test. I didn't mean to look over at Terry's paper when he bent down to pick up his pencil. I didn't mean to write down the answer I saw on his paper for the question I didn't know the answer to. I don't really want to be a cheater. Help me not to do anything like that again, dear God. Amen."

Mother put her arms around Michael and squeezed him close to her. "The Bible says that if we tell God the things we have done wrong, he is always ready to forgive us. So, since you've told him about cheating, I know he has forgiven you. And he'll help you choose to do right, as long as you ask his help every day."

Michael smiled and wiped his eyes. "I feel better now. I guess I ought to tell Miss Scott what I did. Maybe she'll forgive me too. I'll probably get a low grade, but I feel better already."

Smiling, Michael tucked himself down into the covers. "Hey! I just thought of something. I'm hungry now! May I have some of that fruit salad?"

His mother laughed. "Well, that sounds like the Michael that usually lives here. I'm glad the grumpy Michael is gone and the happy one is here again!"

Good Night

Victor Hugo

Good night! Good night!
Far flies the light;
But still God's love
Shall flame above,
Making all bright.
Good night! Good night!

Anything—Even Socks

Joyce K. Ellis

Denny ran down the stairs for breakfast and appeared at the kitchen table all dressed for school.

"Hi, Mom!" he said cheerfully. "What's for breakfast?"

"Socks-a-la-mode," she said. She looked directly at the bare ankle above his left shoe.

"Oh, that." He laughed nervously. "Well, I couldn't find the other sock, and there aren't any clean ones in my drawer. Anyway, these pants are long enough—nobody will ever notice."

"I did," his mother said.

"Yeah, but you're a mother. Mothers are good at that kind of stuff. The kids won't know."

"Whether or not the kids notice your missing sock is not the question." His mom was starting to raise her voice. "You cannot go to school wearing only one sock. You'll get blisters."

"Aw, Mom—"

"Don't 'Aw, Mom' me. Today you

can't find your sock. Yesterday it was your sweater. The day before that, your baseball glove. Either put things where you can find them or learn to hunt better." His mother pointed up the stairs with an unspoken but obvious command.

"I should have painted my ankle blue to match the other sock," he thought as he trudged up the steps. He giggled to himself, imagining his mother's reaction to that!

When he reached his room, he started to look again for his sock. It seemed like a lot of fuss over a sock. But mothers are like that, he thought.

He looked behind his dresser, under the bed, in the closet, in the bathroom. He still couldn't find it. He sat down on his bed.

"I don't know why I can't ever find anything." He was talking to himself—something not at all unusual for Denny. "Everybody calls me 'Scatterbrain,' and I guess they're right. What can I do?"

He sat thinking for several minutes and then said, "I wonder if it would work for this?" He was thinking about what his dad had said the night before.

"God cares about every little detail in the lives of his children," Dad had said, "and he's waiting for us to pray about them."

"I can't think of anything more unimportant to God than a sock," Denny said, glancing at the clock on his dresser. He had only 15 minutes to find that sock, get it on, eat his breakfast, and run for the school bus.

"Lord Jesus," he bowed his head, "I feel kind of silly asking this, but Dad says that the Bible tells us we can ask you to help with anything, no matter how small. Well—could you please help me find my—sock?" He paused. "Thank you, Jesus. Amen."

When he looked up at the clock, he saw that a few minutes already had passed. He searched many of the same places again, determined to find the sock.

"Denny," his mother called. "Hurry or you'll miss your bus."

"I know, Mom," his muffled call came from under the bed. Then he saw it.

Earlier he had just looked quickly under the bed, but now he could see the missing sock wedged between the headboard and the wall.

"Thanks, Lord," he grunted, stretching out on his stomach to reach the blue sock. In a few minutes he was downstairs, gobbling down a piece of toast and some orange juice.

"Where did you find it?" Mom asked.

"I'll tell you about it later, Mom," he said with his mouth full. He ran out the door and waved good-bye.

His mother scratched her head. "Good-bye, Denny. Have a good day!"

Denny raced to the bus stop hoping the driver would wait for him. All the way to school, as Denny stared out the bus window, he thought of some of the other little problems he had been struggling with by himself. He prayed, "God, help me to take better care of all my things." Now he knew that nothing is too small for God. He could pray about anything—even socks.

Teddy's Friend

Mildred Sallee

Teddy looked out the bedroom window into the yard next door. "I didn't know the new neighbors had a little boy," he said. "But I see him sitting on a blanket in the yard."

His mother came to look out the window. "His name is Danny," she said. "I met the family right after they moved in yesterday. Danny is just about your age."

"Why isn't he playing?" Teddy asked. "He's just sitting there." He pressed his nose closer to the window to get a better look. "And what is that heavy, white thing on his leg?"

"That's a cast," his mother explained. "Danny broke his leg a week or so ago. I suppose he's feeling pretty lonely right now."

Teddy watched Danny for a few minutes. He was glad he didn't have a broken leg. It would be terrible not to be able to run and play. "I think I'll go and visit him for a little while," he said.

"That's a wonderful idea," his mother said. "Why don't you take some of your toys with you?"

Teddy didn't answer right away. He hadn't planned to stay long. He had other plans for the day. Then he remembered how lonely Danny looked sitting all alone. "I'll take my set of small cars," he said. "I could take my new box of crayons and a coloring book too." He took the things off the toy shelf and hurried to the yard next door.

Danny smiled when he saw Teddy. "I saw you from my window yesterday," he said. "I hoped you would come over soon."

Teddy sat down on the blanket. "I thought we could play with my cars and maybe color some pictures," he said. He put the things he had brought beside Danny. "We can push up the blanket here and there to make hills and valleys. We can pretend we're driving on a mountain road."

"That's a great idea," Danny agreed.

Teddy was so busy pretending and coloring pictures with Danny he didn't realize it was lunchtime until his mother called him. "I'll come back and play some more after lunch," he promised. "I'll bring my Legos." At the gate, he looked back. Danny didn't look lonely anymore.

Teddy's mother looked up when he entered the kitchen. "You forgot your toys, Teddy," she said.

"Oh, I didn't forget them," Teddy said. "Danny liked a couple of the little cars so much I gave them to him. Besides, I promised to go back after lunch. We're going to build houses with my Legos."

"I'm glad you like your new neighbor," his mother said. "I'm sure Danny is happier too."

Teddy took a big drink of cold milk from the glass his mother had placed before him. "Danny and I will have more fun after the cast comes off his leg." He grinned up at his mother. "I didn't think a boy could have any fun if he couldn't run and play, but I had fun this morning. I guess it's because I found a friend, and friends like to be together no matter what."

The Birthday Party

Helen Kronberg

Mary Blake smiled happily. Next week she would be eight years old. She was going to have a birthday party.

"I wonder if I should invite Ramon," she said to her mother.

"Who is Ramon?" Mother asked.

"He's a new boy in school," Mary replied.

"Don't go overboard. Remember we agreed to keep the party small," Mother reminded her.

Mary twisted a strand of hair thoughtfully. "The other kids might be mad if I invite him. He never plays unless the teacher makes him. He's not much fun."

Her mother nodded.

"It must be awful not to have friends," Mary said.

Mother tapped a pencil on the table. "I see. So what are you going to do?"

"Do you think I should invite him?" Mary asked.

"I think you should decide, Mary. It's your party," Mother replied.

Mary shuffled her feet. Then she said firmly, "I'm going to invite him." She frowned. "But I hope the kids don't laugh at him. And I hope he doesn't bring me a present."

Mother shook her head. "That's a strange thing to say. Why do you hope he doesn't bring a present?"

"I'd have to pretend to like it even if I didn't," Mary answered.

Mother smiled. "We all know how it is to receive a gift we don't especially like. The giver thinks it's nice, so we just say thank you. Anyway, Ramon may surprise you."

The next day, Ramon's happy smile made Mary glad she had decided to invite him. But some of the things her friends said made her wonder. Would she lose her other friends because she wanted to be kind to Ramon?

The day of the party came at last. All the children Mary had invited gathered at her house. All except Ramon.

"Maybe he won't come," one of the guests said.

"I hope he doesn't come," another replied.

But Ramon did come. His hair, black as midnight, was neatly combed. His eyes were like two black cinders in his amber face. He carried a gaily wrapped gift. There was something else. The children could just see it peeking out of his pocket.

"What is that?" Chuck Owens asked.

Ramon pulled it out of his pocket. "At home we have music at parties. I did not know how it is here. So I brought my little wooden flute."

Mary's mother smiled. "How thoughtful!" she said. "Will you play for us?"

Ramon nodded and put the flute to his lips. Music such as the children had never heard filled the air. It was like magic, straight out of a storybook.

When he finished, there was a breathless silence. Then the children applauded, loud and hard. They all crowded around Ramon and looked at his little wooden flute. A few even tried to play it.

"Now I think we'll let Mary open her gifts," her mother said.

Mary sat on the floor. Her gifts were spread all around her. She opened them one by one. She was so excited her fingers trembled on the ribbon bows. At last she came to Ramon's gift. What could it be? she wondered.

It was a little straw horse. She held it up for all to see. It was different. It was beautiful! Only Ramon would ever have given her such a gift.

She smiled at him. "It's the nicest present I ever had in my whole life!" she exclaimed.

Ramon sighed. He smiled shyly.

Why, he's afraid, Mary thought. He was afraid I wouldn't like his gift. He is afraid at school because he doesn't know our games. All his friends are back in his own country. It must be really scary to be all alone.

Mary gathered up the scattered wrappings. She stuffed them into a big box.

"I have an idea," she said. "First we will play a game we all know. Then we will play a game Ramon knows. We will teach him and he can teach us."

"Yay! Great! How about it, Ramon?" the children cheered.

Ramon smiled happily. He looked around at their eager faces. "Great!" he echoed.

Friday Helpers
Ann Hudson Downs

Brad and David lived just around the corner from each other, and the two of them played together almost every day after school. But today they were having trouble deciding what to do.

"Let's play catch," David suggested. "I brought my ball and glove."

"We did that yesterday," Brad reminded him. "Let's ride our bikes."

David shook his head. "We rode our bikes all the way home from school. My legs are tired."

While they were still trying to think of something to do, a woman rolled her wheelchair onto the porch from inside the house next door.

"Who's that?" David asked.

Brad turned to look. "That's Mrs. Brown. Mom says she has come to live with her daughter."

The boys watched as Mrs. Brown looked toward her mailbox out by the street. In a moment, she shook her head from side to side a few times, then rolled back inside.

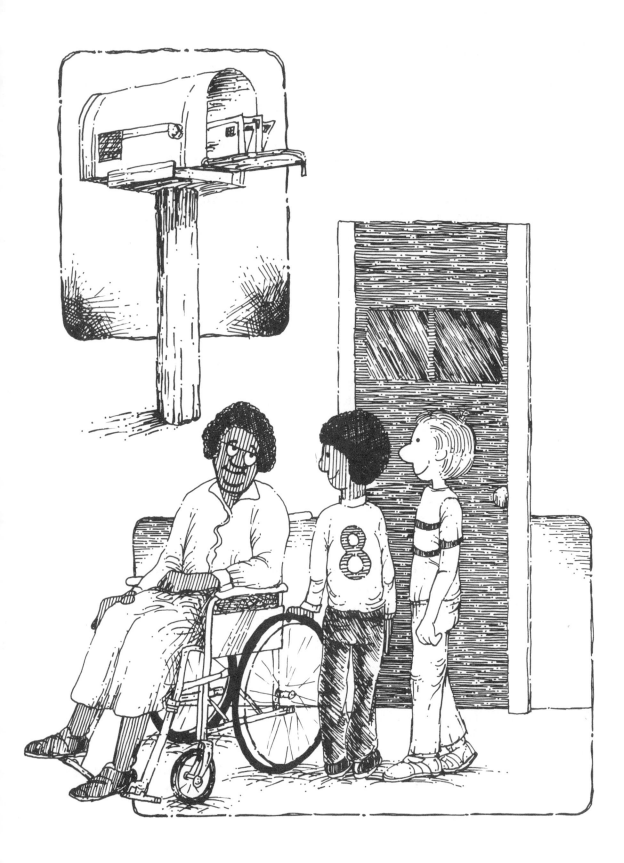

"I think she wants her mail," Brad said. "But she can't get her wheelchair down the steps."

Suddenly David jumped up. "I know what we can do! We can get Mrs. Brown's mail for her."

"Good idea!" Brad said. "But let's ask her first."

When Brad rang the bell, Mrs. Brown opened the door. "My next-door-neighbor, I believe," she said, looking at Brad and smiling.

Brad nodded. "And this is my friend David. We've come to offer our help."

Mrs. Brown looked puzzled, and Brad hurried to explain. "We were wondering if you would like us to bring in your mail."

A pleased look spread over Mrs. Brown's face. "That would be the nicest thing you could do for me. My daughter works later on Fridays, and the day gets rather long. Having my mail would certainly help."

Just then a car passed, and a paper whizzed into the yard. "I'll get your paper," David said.

"And I'll get your mail," Brad called on his way to the mailbox.

Mrs. Brown thanked the boys over and over. Then she reached into her jacket pocket and brought out two quarters. "One for each of you," she said.

"Oh, no. We don't want your money," Brad told her. "We were looking for something to do, and helping you was fun."

David was nodding his head up and down to show that he agreed. "Maybe we can help you some more—especially on Fridays. That is, if you like."

Mrs. Brown smiled. "I would like that very much," she said. "And God bless you," the boys heard her call softly as they turned to hurry home.

Kitten Fight

Catharine Brandt

Danny Sanford carried the bright yellow box into the kitchen. He lifted the cloth cover and picked up the little black kitten inside.

"Here's your new home," he said, stroking the kitten. It made a squeaky mew.

"Mom," Danny said, "Grandmother let me choose the kitten I wanted. She said to call it 'Midnight' because it's all black."

"Put the yellow box behind the kitchen door," his mother told him. "It will be warm there for Midnight."

"Will the kitten know where the box is?" Danny asked. He carried the black kitten to the farthest corner of the kitchen and turned his back on the box. Then he set Midnight down. The kitten made

25

another squeaky mew and scooted for the box.

Danny laughed. "Midnight knows her box," he said.

"Mom, I want to show Midnight to Angie." Angie was in his class, and they walked to school together.

"Don't let Midnight get lost," his mother warned.

"I'll be careful," Danny replied. He carried Midnight snugly against his chest. He could feel the kitten purring as he walked down the block to Angie's house. He wished Angie would see him holding his own kitten. He kept looking up at her house, so he did not see the roller skate on the sidewalk.

Just as Danny decided Angie was not home, he tripped over the roller skate. Down he went. Midnight squirmed out of his arms, scampered across the grass, and disappeared under a big spruce tree.

Danny shouted, "Here, Midnight. Here, Midnight." He ran to the tree and looked under it, but the kitten was not there. He looked all around the neighbor's yard, but Midnight was nowhere in sight. Finally he ran home.

"Mom, I didn't mean to let the kitten get away," he cried. "I tripped. There was nothing to hold onto, and Midnight got away."

Mother went outside and called, "Come, Midnight. Here, kitty, kitty, kitty." But no little black kitten came.

First thing in the morning, Danny ran downstairs to look in the yellow box. The little black kitten was not there.

Sadly Danny ate his breakfast and got ready for school. "I hope Midnight comes back," he said.

When he reached Angie's house, Danny stopped short at what he saw. There on Angie's porch sat a little black kitten.

"Midnight!" Danny exclaimed. He ran up the steps and picked up the kitten. He unzipped his jacket and slipped the kitten inside. Then Angie's front door burst open.

"I saw you, Danny Sanford," Angie cried. "You took my kitten. Bring it right back."

"I won't," Danny yelled. "It's my kitten." Without stopping to explain, he ran home as fast as he could.

"Mom," he called, "here's Midnight."

"You found the kitten!" Mother rejoiced. She took it into her lap and stroked its black fur.

Just then the doorbell rang. "Come in," called Mother.

Angie opened the door. Her jacket was only half on and her face was red. "Mrs. Sanford, Danny took my kitten right off our porch."

"Danny," Mother said, "Angie says the kitten is hers."

The kitten gave its squeaky little mew. Taking courage, Danny said, "I know this is Midnight. Put the kitten down, Mom. If it's Midnight, she'll know about the yellow box behind the door."

Danny held his breath while Mother let the kitten down. It arched its back and stretched its paws. What if it belonged to Angie? Danny knew he should have explained to Angie instead of saying cross words to her that sounded like a fight. Just then the kitten scampered across the kitchen floor and around the door and jumped into the yellow box, where it curled up and shut its eyes.

Danny laughed. "It's Midnight, isn't it, Mom?"

"Yes," agreed Mother, "I think it is Midnight. Now let's explain to Angie. When did you get your kitten, Angie?"

"Last night," Angie said. "It came mewing to our door, and I gave it milk."

Mrs. Sanford put her arm around Angie. "Well, you see, Angie," she said, "Danny's grandmother gave him the kitten yesterday. She let him choose the one he wanted."

"I took it down to show you," broke in Danny, "but you weren't home. I tripped over a roller skate, and the kitten ran away."

"Oh," said Angie slowly. "I don't want the kitten if it really is yours. I didn't know that."

Danny stood still. "I'm glad you took Midnight in last night. I'm sorry you don't have a kitten." He looked at his mother. "Grandma has more kittens. Do you suppose—?"

Mother smiled and nodded her head.

"Angie," Danny said, "let's run and ask your mother if you can have a kitten. Then after school we can go to my grandmother's, and you can choose one for your very own."

The Scary Scritch

Peg Roberts

David yawned as Dad closed the book and tucked the covers up around him and his older brother, Jim. "Good-night," called Dad as he turned out the light and went downstairs.

David snuggled under the warm blankets. This was his favorite time of day, when Dad or Mom read to them from the Bible. Tonight Dad had read about another David, a long-ago shepherd boy who became king.

If I had lived a long time ago, I would have killed wild animals that came to harm my sheep, just the way that other David did. I would have been brave too. "What's that?" David sat straight up in bed, staring into the darkness.

"Scritch, scritch," went something at the window. Suddenly the flickering shadows in the room appeared unfriendly and spooky. David's heart began to pound.

"Jim," he whispered, poking his brother. "Do you hear that?"

"Huh?" asked Jim sleepily. "Hear what?"

"That noise at the window. Something's out there on the roof of the porch."

Jim wiggled and mumbled, "It's probably a tree branch brushing against the window."

"No, it isn't!" David's voice shook. "It sounds like something trying to get in— a wild animal!" All his brave thoughts melted away. "I'm going to climb in bed with Mom and Dad. I'm scared."

"Baby," Jim taunted, sitting up. "That's what little kids do. You're not a little kid any more. Besides, there aren't wild animals around here. I tell you it's nothing, just the wind rattling the window, or a loose shingle, or a tree branch, like I said before. Now go to sleep."

Jim flopped back and shut his eyes. David pulled the covers up tight around his neck. He felt cold inside.

"Scritch, scritch."

David's heart thumped wildly against his ribs. He scooted halfway out of bed, but Jim's taunts rang in his ears. He didn't want to be a baby. He would feel silly running to Mom and Dad if the noise was only a shingle or a tree branch. He rolled over and punched a fist into his pillow so hard the Bible fell off the bedside table. David reached down to pick it up and thought again about the shepherd boy.

That David was not afraid of wild animals, David told himself. He killed the bear ʰⁱᵉᵈ to hurt his sheep. But he was afraid at first. What did he do? He remem-

s with him, David recalled.

me too. I don't need to be afraid, David thought. Wherever I go and), he will be with me. David closed his eyes. "Thank you, God, for near," he prayed.

the edge of the bed and looked around the room. Somehow the med friendly and warm once again.

scritch."

pped out of bed quietly. He tiptoed over to the window and pressed his t the glass. It felt cold. A dark shape moved. David gasped and shrank n he began to laugh.

Softly David opened the window and tugged at a large fluffy ball. It was Marmalade, their orange cat. Marmalade had climbed up on the porch roof and had been scratcning to be let in out of the freezing night air.

"Come on, Marmalade," David said as he shut the window. He crawled back in bed, holding the cat in his arms. "I know just what to do with a wild animal like you."

David pushed Marmalade under the warm covers and was soon fast asleep.

Under the Bed

Eileen Cole

At bedtime, when the lights went out,
I covered up my head,
because I knew that creeps were crawling
underneath my bed.

The big dark place was full of spooks
with eyes big as a cup.
I shivered and I waited
for the things to eat me up.

They clicked their claws and licked
*   their chops*
and waited, still as rocks,
for me to put my feet down,
so they could eat my socks.

Next they might grab me by the toes
and nibble every one.
I got so scared I couldn't move
until the night was done.

But then, the next night, I got brave
and said, "This isn't fair!
You monsters make me sweat and shake,
and you aren't even there!"

I waved my feet beside the bed
because I knew I must,
then I turned on the light and looked—
nothing there but dust!

So now I laugh at bedtime
and wisely shake my head
'cause once I looked for bug-eyed monsters
underneath my bed!

Night Sounds

Betty Brown

When all the day is over
and darkness fills the air,
I listen to the music
of night sounds everywhere.

I hear the leaves that whisper
as little breezes pass,
the happy sound of crickets
that sing there in the grass.

I'm glad for night and darkness,
and time for sleep and rest,
for bedtime prayers together—
that's what I like the best.

Michael's Mitten

Donna Bobb

ichael just couldn't find one of his mittens! He looked under the chair. He looked on the bed. He looked in the closet. But he couldn't find the mitten. Just as Michael was crawling under his bed to look there, his mother came in.

"What are you looking for, Michael?" asked Mother.

"I lost one of my puppet mittens," Michael said, "and they're my favorite ones." He felt like crying.

Mother and Dad helped Michael look for the lost mitten, but it was nowhere to

"Yes," said Dad, "after the paint dries."

When the paint was dry, Dad helped Michael hang the feeder in the big tree. They filled it with seeds.

From the living room window, Michael watched the birds come to eat. His mother and dad joined him. Suddenly Michael saw something bright and yellow moving higher in the tree. It was his mitten!

A little furry face peeked out from under it. "Look," shouted Michael. "My mitten!"

Everyone started laughing at the little squirrel who kept moving the mitten around in his nest. Dad said, "It looks like you've helped more of God's animals today than you thought."

"He seems to like your soft, warm mitten," said Mother.

"Yes," said Michael, "and I'm glad I can help the squirrel stay warm. I have another pair of mittens. He can have that one. OK, Mom?"

That night Michael prayed, "Thank you, God, for giving me my mom and dad, who take good care of me. And thank you for letting me help take care of your birds and squirrels. Amen."

Everything, Praise the Lord!

adapted from Psalm 148
by Carol Greene

Praise God from the heavens!
Angels from on high,
sun and moon and starshine
praise him from the sky.

Praise God from the earth!
Fishes in the sea,
fire and snow and frost
sing of his majesty.

Praise him, furry beasts,
every creeping thing,
every flying bird
shout praises to your king!

Roller Skates

Mae M. Vanderboom

It was Saturday morning and Jean's birthday. As Jean ate breakfast she wondered if her parents would remember the one thing she wanted most.

Sitting in the kitchen, she could hear whispers and laughter coming from the next room. Aunt Kate must be here!

They were talking about her present, she knew. Aunt Kate! That meant it would be a doll. They couldn't give her a doll! Mother knew she hated dolls. But Aunt Kate was always saying that dolls were for little girls, not bats and balls, skateboards, and roller skates. They were bad enough for boys!

Jean heard Aunt Kate leave, saying she would stop in later.

As Jean was finishing her breakfast, her mother and dad came in. They put a beautiful package on the table.

"Happy birthday," her mother said, smiling, and they waited for Jean to unwrap it.

"Thank you," Jean said and looked unhappily at the blue bow and ribbon.

The package was just the right size for that doll Mother had pointed out to her in the store window. And the package was too pretty for the one thing she had wanted more than anything else. She reached for the package but looked down. She didn't want her mother and dad to see the tears that came to her eyes.

Slowly she started to untie the ribbon. Parents just didn't know. They always wanted you to have something pretty. What would she do if it was the doll?

She looked up and made herself smile. I'll like it even if it is a doll, she thought.

A clanging sound came from inside the package. Could it be? Excitedly she tore at the paper. It was! It was the one thing she wanted most of all—a pair of roller skates.

She could hardly wait to get them on. She gave her mother a big hug and her dad a big kiss and darted out to the back steps.

"They're the nicest skates I ever saw," she told them, as they watched her from the kitchen door. "I'm glad Tom taught me how to skate."

When Jean stood up, the skates started rolling at once—around the house, to the front sidewalk, and down the street. It was wonderful to feel herself gliding so smoothly over the cement.

They don't stick like Tom's, she thought to herself.

As she flew along, she looked over into the yard next door. I wonder if Tom will see me, she thought.

She went to the end of the street. When she came back, Tom was playing catch with his ball against the side of his house.

and come too," she called. "We'll have a race." Was she being selfish? she wondered.

Slowly Tom went for his old rusty skates and put them on. He started up the sidewalk, but the rollers stuck. He could hardly make one trip to the end of the block and back in the time Jean made two.

"Let's play sailboat," he called at last, making a sail of his sweater to catch the wind.

That didn't help him much.

Jean looked down at Tom's old rusty skates. She remembered when they were new and shiny. That was when she had learned to skate on them. She looked down at her own shining rollers. How could she give them up—even for a short time?

At the end of the street she stopped to watch Tom. He was trying hard to keep up.

"Here comes the freight train," he called, chugging noisily when he saw her watching him.

Jean went to her porch steps to wait. When Tom came up, she had her skates off. She handed them to him.

"Let me have yours. I'll be the freight train for a while."

"Oh, no," said Tom. "This is your birthday."

"Go ahead, put them on," she said. She watched the pleasure on Tom's face as he put on the new skates and started rolling smoothly down the street.

"They're great," he called back to her.

Jean felt all happy inside. This was as much fun as rolling along on them herself!

"New skates!" he called, seeing Jean. "Come on over."

Jean laughed back and sped on.

If I stop now, she thought, he will want me to let him use them because he let me use his.

Up and down the sidewalk she flew, waving to him each time she passed. It was very exciting and great fun.

Tom sat down on his doorstep to watch her. Each time Jean passed him she felt less happy. "Get your skates

Grandmother's Little Game
Claire Lynn

Grandma had just finished reading Karen her favorite story from the Bible. Karen was snuggled up close. She put her head on Grandma's shoulder.

"Gram," she said, "I love Jesus, but I'm not always happy like you. How can I be happy, Gram?"

Grandma patted Karen's brown curls. "I will tell you how to be happy," she said, "but first I will ask you to do three things for me."

"All right." Karen sat up straight. This was like a game. "What three things?"

"First, find someone who is sick and take that person some flowers. Next, think of someone who doesn't have many things and give him something of yours. Third, find someone who is tired and do something to help.

"Do these three things now, and when you come back, I will tell you how you can be happy."

"I'll start now," Karen said, jumping down from beside her grandmother. "Let me see.... Rosalee Perkins has a sprained ankle. I could take her some flowers."

In the vacant lot next door, she picked a bouquet of wild flowers. After getting permission from her mother, she crossed the street and rang Rosalee's doorbell. Mrs. Perkins answered.

"I've brought flowers for Rosalee," Karen said.

"Why, how sweet of you, Karen," Mrs. Perkins exclaimed. "What a thoughtful little girl you are."

Rosalee clapped her hands. "Oh, how nice, Karen," she called from her bedroom. "Please come in and talk to me. I miss playing outdoors."

Karen stayed a while with her friend. What fun they had laughing and talking together. Then Karen remembered. "I have to go now, Rosalee. I have two things to do."

"Come back soon," Rosalee begged. "It's nice to have you visit me."

"Yes, please do come back," Mrs. Perkins added. "Rosalee hasn't been so happy since she hurt her ankle."

"Thank you," Karen smiled. "I'll come again."

Karen ran home. She was thinking of Grandma's second request, "Think of someone who doesn't have many things and give him something of yours."

There's Stevie, she thought. He doesn't have many toys at all.

In her room she looked at her toys. Stevie wouldn't like dolls or a jump rope, but he might like a book.

She took down a storybook full of pictures. I'm sure he'll like this one, she thought.

Stevie was playing in front of his house, drawing with a stick in the dust. He looked up and smiled at her as she opened the gate.

"Hi, Karen, where are you going?" he asked.

"I came to see you," she answered.

Stevie looked pleased.

"I brought this for you." She held out the little book.

"For me?" He took it eagerly. Sitting down on the steps, he began to turn the pages and study the pictures.

Karen sat down beside him and explained each picture. "There's Peter in his boat catching fish. That's the little boy who gave his bread and fish to Jesus."

When they reached the last picture, Stevie closed the book and held it out to Karen.

"I'm glad you brought your book to show me," he said.

"Oh," said Karen, "I brought it to give it to you. It's yours now."

"To keep?" He couldn't believe it.

"Yes."

At last he seemed to understand. He hugged the book and his eyes were bright with pleasure.

"Thank you, Karen, I love it. I never had a book all my very own. Please come back and tell me all the stories, will you?"

Karen promised she would and skipped off toward home.

"Get ready for lunch, Karen," Mother called to her as she burst into the house.

Karen ran to wash her hands. Mom looks tired, she thought as she rinsed away the soap.

Back in the kitchen, she patted her mother's arm. "I can set the table for you, Mom," she said.

Mother gave her a quick little hug. "There's a sweet girl," she said.

After lunch Karen cleared the table, then, with a big towel tied around her waist, she wiped the dishes. She and Mother sang together as they worked.

After they had finished, Mother went to rest. Karen hung the towels up to dry. Then she went to find Grandma, who was mending a shirt.

Karen felt all warm and good inside. She stood for a moment beside Gram, watching the little silver needle flashing in and out.

"Well, Karen, have you finished my three commands?" Gram asked.

"Yes, Grandma."

"And now you want to know how to be happy?"

Karen was quiet a while, but her eyes sparkled and she smiled a little.

"I think I know, Gram."

Grandma looked up. "What's that?" she grinned. "You think you know?"

"Well," said Karen slowly, "when I forget about making *myself* happy and start to make *other* people happy, I get happy myself without trying."

Grandma nodded. "So you guessed our little game. Yes, the greatest happiness of all is found in showing love to others."

Karen yawned sleepily. It had been a happy morning. She kicked off her shoes and curled up contentedly on the sofa beside Grandma for an afternoon nap.

The Circus Balloon
Penny Jans

Jamie proudly carried his balloon from the auditorium. He looked around and saw other balloons bobbing up and down above the heads of the crowd of people. He looked up, his eyes following the long string tied to his wrist. There above him was his balloon, swaying in the slight breeze. The blue mouse inside the clear bubble seemed to smile down at him.

For a moment a worried feeling flashed through Jamie's mind. Would Mother be angry? She had warned him to spend his money wisely. "Remember, Jamie, the balloons are expensive and don't last long. Maybe you should buy a different souvenir at the circus." Jamie had nodded his head in agreement.

But when the balloon man appeared, Jamie completely forgot Mother's advice. There were the balloons, hundreds of them, floating above the man's head. Many of his classmates had crowded around to buy one. Jamie had quickly pushed forward too.

His friend Hank had said, "I'm getting a monkey on a string instead of a balloon. Balloons pop!" Jamie had

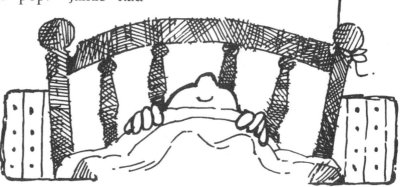

heard him, but he wanted a balloon. His balloon wouldn't pop. He would be very careful with it.

As Jamie rode home on the bus, he clutched his balloon close to him. He would protect it from anything that might pop it. He sighed with relief when the bus finally arrived back at the school.

Once again a worried feeling flashed through Jamie's mind as he saw Mother waiting for him. But when he walked toward her, with his balloon in hand, she smiled at him.

"Oh, I see you bought a balloon," she said.

All the excitement of the day burst out of him. He told her about the

clowns, the lions, and each act of the circus. He repeated the story at dinner for the rest of the family and proudly displayed the balloon.

That night Jamie tied his balloon to his bedpost. When he said his prayers, he looked up at it. He fell asleep with pleasant thoughts of circus acts and high-flying balloons.

In the morning, he opened his eyes expecting to see the mouse balloon smiling down at him. But it wasn't there. Jamie lay still for a moment, his eyes searching the ceiling above him. Suddenly, he sat up.

There was his balloon on the floor beside the bed. It was much smaller than the night before. Tears came to his eyes.

Just then Mother appeared in the doorway.

Jamie picked up the balloon and held it high. He let it go, but it fell to the floor again. "What happened to my balloon?" he asked.

"Some of the helium must have leaked out in the night," Mother replied.

"Blow it up again," Jamie cried.

"I can blow it up for you, Jamie, but it won't float in the air. It was filled with a special gas called helium to make it float." Mother put her arms around him and said, "I'm sorry about your balloon, Jamie."

"I should have bought a monkey on a string," said Jamie.

"Sometimes we decide to do something that later doesn't seem like a very wise choice. But next time you will be able to make a better decision," said Mother.

Jamie looked at his mother. "I'll just blow the balloon back up to play with. It won't float, but at least the mouse is still smiling."

Jenny's Droopy Tulip
Martha P. Johnson

Jenny hooked her toes under the rung of the chair in front of her and wiggled. Choir practice was usually fun, but today Mrs. Bell was taking time to talk about the program they were going to give at the nursing home.

Finally she said, "Now let's practice the flower song."

Jenny, Bob, Alice, and Tommy filed to the front and picked up huge cardboard flowers. Jenny's was a red tulip. It had a wooden yardstick taped to the back to make it stand up straight. But the tape was coming unstuck, and Jenny's flower began to droop in the middle of the song. The children giggled, and Jenny's face grew very red. She stopped singing and tried to prop the flower back up.

Mrs. Bell sighed and signaled for the music to stop. "That's all we have time for today. Let's see if we can get the flowers to stay together before our program on Wednesday night."

Chairs scraped as everyone scurried for the door.

"Not it! Not it!" they shouted as they raced outside for a game of tag before going home.

"Not it!" shouted Jenny, and the red tulip lay forgotten on the floor.

On Wednesday night, Jenny squeezed into a car with the other children for the short ride to the nursing home. The children sang and told jokes as they rode. But when they left the car and started walking toward the nursing home, suddenly everyone was very quiet.

A smiling nurse met them at the door. All the children crowded into the silent hallway. The walls were green, and their feet made whispering sounds on the shiny floor.

"Sure smells funny in here," muttered Bob.

But Jenny wasn't thinking about the smell, though it reminded her of the doctor's office. She was thinking about the funny feeling in her stomach and wondering why her hands felt so cold.

They stopped at the entrance to a large room. Jenny peeked inside. There were so many people there! Some sat in rocking chairs, some in wheelchairs. Most of them wore bathrobes and slippers.

"Let's pray and ask God to help us before we go in to sing," Mrs. Bell said.

Just as Jenny bowed her head, she remembered the red tulip. She had forgotten to fix the tape on it!

Mrs. Bell prayed, "Jesus, please help us make the people happy with our program. Amen."

"And please don't let my tulip fall down," Jenny added quietly to herself.

There wasn't time to do anything else. All the people were looking at them as Mrs. Bell sat at the piano. Jenny guessed that the others felt as funny as she did. Her voice sounded squeaky, and she felt as if she were singing all alone. At last the first song ended, and a few people clapped.

Mrs. Bell had warned them that the people might not feel well enough to clap. But Jenny knew the song had been terrible, and she wanted to run away when Mrs. Bell called for the flower song.

Jenny, Bob, Alice, and Tommy's flowers held their heads up high as the song began. But in the middle of the first line, Jenny's tulip began to droop. Alice giggled. Jenny closed her eyes and clutched the yardstick tighter. She could hear some children behind her laugh. As the red tulip slowly pulled loose from the yardstick and dropped closer to the floor, more people began to laugh. The nurses giggled. The patients in the rocking chairs and wheelchairs laughed. Even Mrs. Bell stopped playing the piano because she was laughing so hard. Finally Jenny laughed too, as the red tulip slid slowly to the floor.

Somehow, when everyone had stopped laughing, the tight feeling in Jenny's stomach was gone. Everyone else seemed to feel better too. The boys and girls sang out clearly, just as they had at practice. The people watching smiled and tapped their feet. And they all clapped when the program was over.

When they went down the long hall again, Jenny thought she could still hear the clapping and see the warm smiles.

Mrs. Bell gave her a hug. "I felt angry at first when I saw that you hadn't fixed your flower, Jenny. But what happened made everyone relax and have a good time. It was really for the best."

On her way to the car, Jenny thought, Jesus did answer my prayer. He made something good come from my mistake.

When Will the Sun Shine?   Sharon Ihnen

Splish! Splash! Plop! Splish! Splash! Plop!

Andy MacDonald rubbed his nose up and down the slippery cold window. Splish! Splash! Plop! the raindrops said as they hit the window and wiggled down the glass. Andy blew his breath on the window and made it misty. Then he rubbed his nose up and down the glass, making little squeak-squeak noises. Now his nose felt bumpy and numb from the cold, and the fogged-over window was full of long nose marks. The rain said Splish! Splash! Plop!

Andy's mother said, "Please don't rub on the window, Andy. Why don't you go and play with your new paint set?"

Andy frowned at the rain. "I want to go outside, Mom. Is it ever going to stop raining?"

It had been raining for five whole days now, and Andy was tired of staying in the house. He had drawn all the

pictures he could think of out of his head. He had picked up all the lost nails around the tool bench and put them in the right boxes. He had looked at all his books. Now he wanted to go outside and play with his big brown dog, Ruffy. He wanted to stretch out flat in the grass and say Hi! to the sun.

But there wasn't any sun—there hadn't been for five whole days now. And Ruffy just kept lying in his red doghouse with his head on his paws and his eyes all sad. Andy could see him now through the wet, rainy window.

"Won't the rain ever stop, Mom?" Andy asked again. "When will it ever stop?"

His mother said, "Of course the rain will stop sometime soon—maybe tomorrow. It always rains in the springtime, Andy. That's because God knows that the flowers and grass and trees are very thirsty. So God sends them the rain to make them grow."

"But I get thirsty too, Mom, and I don't want all this much water!"

Andy's mother laughed. Then she helped him find his favorite old train set in the back of his closet. For the rest of the afternoon he was Engineer Andy. He went racing over bridges and chasing through the tunnels, and he blew his whistle at all the towns as he went rushing past. But he didn't forget about the rain. Splish! Splash! Plop!

That night at dinner, Andy was very quiet. He chewed on his drumstick and poked his peas around and around on his plate. Usually he liked to tell Dad all about his day and about the brave things he and Ruffy had done outside. But tonight there wasn't anything to tell. Nothing at all. So Andy didn't say much.

Splish! Splash! Plop! said the rain.

Andy really was beginning to be a little bit afraid that the rain wasn't going to stop. Maybe he wouldn't be able to run in the grass and say Hi! to the sun tomorrow. Or the next tomorrow. Maybe the sun had gone away and wouldn't come back.

Bedtime came—the cuckoo clock said so. Andy was tired, not sleepy-tired, but tired of the rain. After he had said his prayers, he lay under the covers listening hard. Splish! Splash! Plop! said the rain on the roof. Andy turned over on his stomach and pulled the pillow over his head so he couldn't hear the rain. After a while he fell asleep.

When Andy woke up the next morning, he poked his head out from under the pillow and listened as hard as he could. He heard some birds having a fight in the apple tree. He heard Ruffy barking. He heard his mother singing in the kitchen. But he didn't hear any rain!

"No rain, no rain, no rain on my windowpane," Andy said out loud. He sat up and pulled back the blue curtains. He blinked and blinked because the sun was big and round and yellow in his eyes.

Andy jumped out of bed and dressed so fast that he put his shirt on backwards. He scrubbed at his face until the mirror in the bathroom said his cheeks and nose were red. He ran down all the stairs, and he almost made it out the

back door onto the porch before his mother grabbed his belt.

"Hey there, Speedy, breakfast first," she said.

Andy ate faster than he had ever eaten. "'Scused please?" he gulped, putting the last bite of pancake in his mouth and sliding off his chair at the same time.

"OK, go on outside," laughed Andy's mom.

Andy banged the screen door and took the steps two at a time. He hopped three times on the gravel in the driveway and threw a stick at the apple tree before Ruffy found him and jumped at him. Down they both went. They rolled and squirmed and squealed. Ruffy growled and pushed his nose into Andy's stomach. Andy laughed and grabbed Ruffy's ears. Over and over they rolled in the sunshine on the warm green grass.

Then Andy ran to the corner of the yard where the grass was the longest. He flopped on his back in the grass and stretched his arms and legs out. Ruffy ran around him in circles and barked.

Andy put his head way back with his face straight up into the sun. When he closed his eyes tight, the sun made red dancing spots on the insides of his eyes. Andy laughed and yelled, "Hi, sun! Hi, sun!" And the big yellow sun smiled right back into his eyes and over his face.

All day Andy was outside. All day the sun was there with him. That night when he climbed into his bed in the corner, he was really tired, tired in his legs and his arms and in his eyes. But before he went to sleep, he got up on his knees and pulled the curtain back so he could see the stars. He looked right up into the sky and said softly, "Thank you, God, for the sun. Thank you for Ruffy. Thank you for the grass."

He thought for a minute. Then he said quickly, "And thank you for the rain that makes the grass grow. But please don't let it rain tomorrow."

When God Made the World

Elizabeth Friedrich

When God made the world,
   (trace circle with finger in air)
he said, "Let there be light."
   (outstretch arms)
Then day was created
   (arms overhead)
and followed by night.
   (arms down)
God made the land.
   (extend hands)
He made the oceans too.
   (make waves with fingers)
He even grew grass
   (raise hands slowly)
and seeds just for you.
   (point)
God made moon
   (cup hands)
and stars,
   (twinkle fingers)
and the sun so bright
   (arms overhead)

just so you wouldn't mix up
day and night.
   (shake head no)
God made whales to swim
   (swimming motion)
and sparrows so free.
   (flying motion)
He made them all for you
and for me.
   (point)
Ponies to ride
   (riding motion)
and puppies to love,
   (pat pretend puppy in arms)
they each come to us from
God up above.
   (point above)
But God's favorite creation
   (outstretch arms)
still hadn't arrived
   (shake head no)
till he made boys and girls
to stay by his side.
   (put hands down by sides)

A Problem for Robby

Lois Kaufmann

Robby Blake looked up as he came down the street from school. There on the porch sat his father in his wheelchair.

"Hi, Rob, old pal," Dad greeted him. "I thought you would bring Mike along home tonight."

"I will, Dad—sometime," Robby answered. "Right now I'm hungry. What's there to eat?"

"Graham crackers and milk," Dad answered. "I'm planning to make apple dumplings so they'll be warm for supper. How does that sound?"

"Good," Robby answered through a mouthful of graham crackers. He took his snack up to his room.

Mr. Blake had a puzzled look on his face. "I wonder," he said slowly. "I think I'll take a little run down the street." He started the motor on his wheelchair, went down the ramp, and started down the street toward the house where Mike had lived for the past few weeks.

Upstairs, Robby leaned his elbows on the windowsill. "Everybody else's dad works," he muttered. "My dad cooks and washes and irons. What would Mike think if he knew my dad bakes pies and stuff like that? He always talks about his dad being a big businessman." He kicked his shoe across the room and slipped into his running shoes. "Funny," he thought, "I never thought anything of Dad staying home while Mom works until Mike moved in."

While Robby was changing clothes and working on his kite, his father was humming to himself as he rode down the street. He saw a boy idly tossing stones into a fishpond.

The boy looked up. "Hey! That's a neat outfit you have there!" he exclaimed.

Mr. Blake stopped his chair. "You must be Mike," he said.

"I am. Who are you?"

"I'm Robby Blake's father."

"Really? He never told me you have such a neat outfit. Does it really run by itself? How come you're in a wheelchair?"

"My back was hurt in an accident. My legs are paralyzed, so now I get around on wheels," Mr. Blake said. "Well, I'd better get moving if I'm going to have apple dumplings for supper. Want to come along and help me?"

"Sure do!" Mike exclaimed eagerly.

"Change your clothes and ask if it's OK while I finish my ride. Then I'll stop by for you."

"My folks don't get home until six. I'm here by myself. I'll be ready in a second." Mike scooted into the house, and by the time Mr. Blake was back he was waiting impatiently at the gate.

"This is going to be fun," Mike said as he trotted beside the wheelchair. Up the ramp they went, and into the house.

"I have the crust mixed and ready to roll out," Mr. Blake said. "Can you do that?"

"You mean you'll let *me* do it?" Mike asked. He washed his hands and grabbed the rolling pin.

Mr. Blake watched a moment. "Nice going. Now roll the other way so it spreads out even."

While Mike was rolling out the crust, Mr. Blake sliced apples into a bowl and mixed them with brown sugar, cinnamon, and butter.

"This is fun," Mike said. "Lots more fun than sitting and waiting for my dad and mom to come home. There's nothing to do when I'm home by myself."

"Robby needs someone to play with," Mr. Blake said. Just then Robby came from his room with his finished kite.

"Mike!" he exclaimed, blinking his eyes. "Mike—Dad—what's going on here?"

"I'm helping to make apple dumplings. Don't they look good?"

"But how—" Robby began.

"I took a little stroll down the street in my chair," explained Mr. Blake. "I saw Mike sitting all lonesome-like, so I invited him to help me."

"It's great having a dad to do things with," Mike said, licking his fingers. "You're lucky, Robby. My dad is at the office most of the time. He hardly ever has time to do things with me."

Into the oven went the apple dumplings. "As soon as they are done, we will put the meat loaf and potatoes in to bake," Mr. Blake said.

"We'll probably have frozen dinners again," Mike said, turning up his nose. "My folks don't get home in time to really cook."

"Eat with us," Robby said eagerly. Mike looked at Mr. Blake.

"We made an extra dumpling—just in case," smiled Mr. Blake. "Robby will wash another potato, I'm sure."

"You better believe it!" Robby said, laughing. "This will be fun. Everything will be ready when Mom comes from work. Won't she be happy!" Robby put his arm across his father's shoulder. "Thanks, Dad," he whispered in his ear. "You're super!"

What's the Difference?

Lois Holm

Kathy Martin stood in front of her bedroom mirror looking at herself sadly. She thought she was about the funniest-looking third grader in the whole world.

Her blond hair was short and curly. She wanted it long and straight. But that wasn't the worst part.

She groaned out loud, "Such stupid, funny-looking knees!" She tried to straighten them by stretching her legs. It didn't help. Her knees curved in, almost touching each other. She groaned again.

"What are you groaning about?" asked her big sister, looking up from her geography book.

Kathy cried, "Look at my funny knees! How will I look in a swimsuit?"

Her sister laughed. "If that's the worst problem you ever have, you're lucky. You should be trying to pass a geography test."

"You don't have to laugh," yelled Kathy. She ran from the room, down the stairs, and out of the house.

She ran to the corner house where her friend Susan lived. Susan was sitting on the front steps playing with her family of dolls.

"Oh, Susan," moaned Kathy, "I have the worst problem. I have such funny knees. Yours aren't stupid looking. Just look at mine!"

Susan looked. "They're not that bad, Kathy." Then she frowned. "You're lucky you don't have crazy-colored hair like mine." She leaned forward. "Look at how many different colors it has."

Kathy thought it did look a little strange, all streaked with brown and blond colors. But she could dye it, Kathy thought.

Susan said, "I really don't care, though, because my children don't mind." She patted her baby doll and said, "Don't worry about your knees."

Kathy walked slowly down the street. Sure, Susan could say, "Don't worry." She didn't have funny knees.

She was thinking so hard that she bumped into a bike and heard an angry voice say, "Watch where you're going!"

She looked up and saw Mike Harper straddling his bike, looking at her crossly. His baseball and mitt had spilled to the sidewalk.

"Mike, let me see your knees," said Kathy suddenly.

"What?" cried Mike in surprise. "What for?"

He was wearing shorts, so Kathy stared at his legs. "Your knees are perfect," she wailed. "Everybody has perfect knees but me."

Mike said, "Huh! What's so bad about that? I have a red birthmark on my neck that I can't even cover up with my shirt. How would you like that?"

He picked up his mitt and ball and rode off shouting, "But I don't care. It doesn't keep me from playing ball."

Kathy looked down at her knees sadly and walked on until she came to her best friend Janey's house. Janey was scrubbing hard on her bike. She loved that bike more than almost anything else.

Kathy ran up to her and said, "Oh, Janey. I have the worst problem, and nobody will help me."

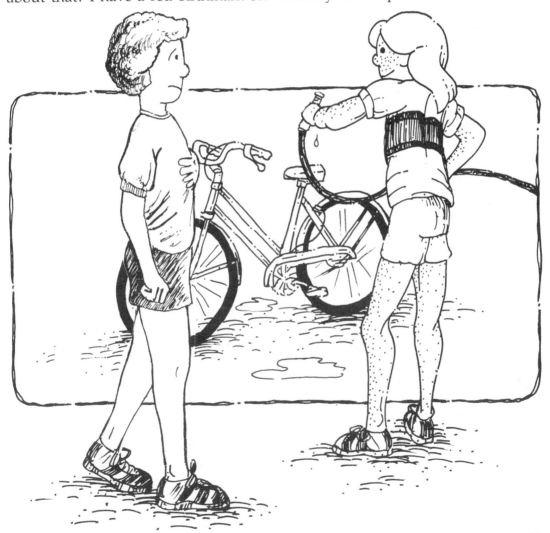

"What's wrong?" asked Janey.

"I have funnier knees than anybody. Look!"

While Janey looked, Kathy studied Janey's knees. "Yours are just perfect," she said. But she thought Janey looked sad.

Janey said, "I don't think your knees are funny," and scrubbed harder on her bike wheel, splashing water on her shoes.

She was silent so long that Kathy said, "Janey, what's the matter? Is something else wrong with me?"

Janey shook her head. "Not with you. With me!"

Kathy was surprised. "You?"

Janey nodded and turned to Kathy. "Look at all my freckles! I have so many there's hardly room for skin," and she began to cry.

Kathy looked at Janey's face. It was full of freckles. I never really noticed before, thought Kathy. Poor Janey.

Janey was sobbing. "I've tried all kinds of things—mother's vanishing cream and sandpaper and everything. Nothing helps," she wailed.

"Don't cry," said Kathy. "It doesn't really matter. I like you anyway. Everybody does. Freckles don't make any difference."

She looked around then and said, "Besides, they don't keep you from riding your bike."

Janey just cried harder. Kathy felt very sad and tried to think of something cheerful to say. "Freckles aren't so bad, Janey. You could have something worse like—like—no face at all."

Janey looked up and smiled a tiny smile. "Oh, Kathy. Nobody has no face at all. That would be awful."

Kathy was glad to see her friend smile. She said, "It would even be worse than funny knees, wouldn't it?"

Janey nodded, wiping her tears on the back of her hand, while Kathy studied her own knees.

Kathy said, "I guess my knees aren't so bad. I'd rather have them than none at all." She grinned. "Besides, they don't keep me from riding my bike either. I'll get it. Let's go for a ride."

Tassy, Come Home

Sue Richterkessing

"Oooooo," sang the wind. "Crackle, pop, crackle, pop," roared the thunder. "Pitter, pat, pitter, pat," tinkled the rain.

"Squeak, creak, squeak, creak," sounded Mary Elizabeth's chair as she rocked back and forth. What a good night to be inside with Mom and Dad and Terry. But Mary Elizabeth was not happy. Tassy, her kitten, was lost in the spring storm.

"Don't worry," said her mother, "she'll come home when the storm is over."

"Don't worry," said Terry, "maybe she'll find a nice, dry place to hide from the storm."

"Don't worry," said her father. "Come sit on my lap and I will tell you a story about a small gray kitten named Tassy."

"Oh, Daddy," cried Mary Elizabeth, "don't tell me a story about Tassy now. I just want my kitten!"

Then Mary Elizabeth began to remember: God loves me. God loves Tassy. I don't know where Tassy is, but God knows.

"Dear God," prayed Mary Elizabeth. "I miss Tassy. I'm afraid something has happened to her. Please take care of Tassy and bring her home to me."

"Ding, dong, ding," went the doorbell. When Mary Elizabeth's father opened the door, there stood Mr. Sturm, their next-door neighbor.

"I think I have something that belongs to you," he said. "I left my boots sitting on my porch when I came home from the firehouse. They were wet from the storm, so I just brought them inside to dry out. But was I surprised when one of the boots began making a funny sound. Can you guess what it was?"

Mary Elizabeth peeked inside. There, curled up in the bottom of Mr. Sturm's boot, was a sleepy little Tassy. Mary Elizabeth picked Tassy out of the boot. Tassy blinked her eyes and snuggled into Mary Elizabeth's arms.

"Thank you, Mr. Sturm, for bringing Tassy home," said Mary Elizabeth. "And thank you, God, for taking care of Tassy—and for answering my prayer."

Every Dog Should Have a Boy

Betty Lou Mell

"Come on, girl—come on," Jerry coaxed.

He stood on tiptoe and leaned over the fence to scratch the dog's pointed ear. The dog stood on her hind legs and licked Jerry's mitten. Jerry rummaged in his lunch and pulled out a cookie.

"Here you are, girl," Jerry smiled as the dog chomped the cookie and wagged her orange tail for more. One more scratch at the dog's ear, then Jerry hurried off to school. The dog followed along the fence, then stood with front paws pressed against the wire, watching.

If that dog were his, he'd walk it every day. Jerry knew he'd never have a dog though—because of his sister's al-

lergy. Every day he stopped on his way to school and pretended for a little while that the dog was his. He glanced back and saw Tim Nichols stop at the fence. Oh, well, guess it's OK if Tim pets the dog too, he decided, then hurried toward school.

But, as he stopped to pet the dog one day, Mrs. Bloom's back door suddenly opened. "Young man!" Mrs. Bloom called. "Wait a minute!"

Jerry glanced both ways along the alley and wondered why she wanted to see him. He scraped his boot along the snow and watched as Mrs. Bloom stumbled across the yard, wrapping a scarf about her neck.

"I don't like it one bit that you've been letting my dog loose!" she growled.

"But, ma'am—" Jerry stammered.

"I see you out here! It took me an hour to find her yesterday—in this freezing weather!" Mrs. Bloom shook her finger and glared.

Jerry's face turned red, and he blinked to stop the tears. Tim Nichols came walking along the alley. He glanced at Jerry and Mrs. Bloom, then stopped.

"The next time I see you even stopping at my fence, I'll call your parents!" Mrs. Bloom threatened.

"But, ma'am—" Jerry stammered. "I didn't—"

Tim Nichols hurried toward school.

"That's enough!" Mrs. Bloom shouted. "Get along now, and don't let me see you around here again!"

Jerry stumbled through the snow.

Behind him, he heard the dog whimper. As Jerry wiped his mitten across his nose, Tim grinned at him. "I'm glad she caught you instead of me."

"She thinks I let her dog out of the yard," Jerry replied sadly. "Hey, wait! Did you let her loose?"

Tim shrugged. "I can't reach over the fence like you can."

"You let me take the blame! Why didn't you tell her it was you?" Jerry asked angrily.

"And get into trouble?" Tim laughed and ran into the school.

From then on Jerry walked to school along High Street, and every time he saw Tim Nichols, he thought of Tim's dirty trick. And every time Tim saw Jerry, he hurried away as though he were afraid of him.

Jerry missed the dog and wondered if the orange dog missed him too. He could imagine her waiting by the fence—alone and lonely. Then one day Mrs. Bloom called to him out her front door.

"Young man!" she called.

Jerry stopped in his tracks. His heart pounded and his stomach churned. He looked both ways along the street.

"Come on!" she called.

Jerry hurried up the walk.

"I have something to show you," Mrs. Bloom said as she led the way to the kitchen.

Beside the stove, the big orange dog lay on a rug. As Jerry approached, her tail thumped loudly against the floor. Jerry saw tiny tails wagging as three orange puppies cuddled up to their mother. Jerry's eyes nearly popped, and he giggled as the puppies began to tug at his pantlegs. "Oh—they're so cute," Jerry beamed.

"I'm sorry I lost my temper with you. But Lady was going to have puppies, and I didn't want anything to happen to her," Mrs. Bloom said softly. "To make amends, I'd like to give you one."

Jerry trailed his fingers over the puppies and thought of his sister. His eyes filled with tears, and he kept staring down so Mrs. Bloom wouldn't see. "I'd

really like that, but my sister—" He swallowed hard and rubbed his nose. "She's allergic to dogs."

Mrs. Bloom nodded. "You're welcome to stop and see Lady any time, so long as you don't let her out of the yard."

"Oh, no," Jerry replied. "I'd never do that."

Jerry stood and looked at Lady. She looked back at him and wagged her tail—they were still friends.

"Seems she really likes you," Mrs. Bloom said. "I suppose every boy should have a dog—maybe every dog should have a boy. Maybe you could walk her once in a while. On a leash, of course. I'd be glad to pay you."

"You don't have to pay me!" Jerry laughed. He felt like running and jumping and crying all at the same time. Instead, he hugged Lady's neck. "Can I walk her today?" he asked excitedly. "Just a little way. She probably needs exercise."

Mrs. Bloom laughed. "All right—stop after school."

Jerry paused at the door. "I know someone who might want a puppy."

Mrs. Bloom smiled. "I'd like to find them all good homes."

"I'll find out for sure," Jerry promised.

Tim Nichols couldn't believe his ears! "You're going to tell Mrs. Bloom I want a puppy?" he stammered. "After I got you in trouble?"

"Aw, forget it, Tim, that's over. And just because I can't have a puppy, that's no reason you shouldn't." Jerry shrugged.

"I thought you hated me," Tim replied.

"Well, I don't." Jerry started walking, then he turned and called, "Well, don't you want to see the puppies?"

"Sure!" Tim laughed. He grabbed his books and hurried after Jerry.

The Boy Who Loved the Wind

Betty Lou Mell

Johnny Carpenter was not a strange boy. He liked to run and jump like everyone else. Sometimes he made his bed, and sometimes he didn't. He liked popcorn and cinnamon toast and even spinach, but what he loved most was the wind.

He liked to watch birds fly on the wind. He liked to watch leaves dance in the wind. He liked to watch the wheat blowing in the wind. Sometimes he climbed up into his tree house and closed his eyes just to feel the wind on his face.

"Johnny!" his mother called. "Time to eat!"

Johnny climbed down. "I'll be right back," he whispered as he closed the screen door behind him. And the wind waited. It whistled under the door, it blew the clothes on the line, and it rattled the windows. It waited for Johnny to come out. As soon as Johnny had eaten, he ran outside, calling, "Bye, Mom."

"Where are you going?" his mother asked.

"To the top of the hill," Johnny called.

He ran through the tall grass, and the wind blew in his hair. He spread his fingers and tried to catch the wind as he ran, but the wind laughed and just kept blowing. At the top of the hill, Johnny stopped. He cupped his hands to his mouth and shouted, "Hello!" Then he listened. The wind carried his shout across the hills and back to him. Johnny was not alone.

One day he made a kite and ran to the hilltop. He put the kite on the ground and began to run. The kite lifted and zigzagged across the field. But when Johnny stopped running, the kite stopped flying. He looked around. All the trees were still, and the grass wasn't moving. Nothing played with his hair, and everything was quiet.

"Hey, wind!" he called. "Where are you?"

But the wind didn't answer. Johnny sat on the ground and waited. He watched as ants crawled through the grass and grasshoppers jumped on his jeans. Still Johnny waited.

He saw the garbage truck go up the lane. He saw the mailman stop at every box. Still Johnny waited. By the end of the day, the wind had not come. He picked up his kite and walked slowly down the hill.

That night he listened for the wind at his window, but it did not come. The next day, he watched and waited, but it did not come.

Even his mother and father missed it. They sat on the porch and said, "I wish there were a breeze."

"We need rain," his father said.

That night, Johnny knelt to say his prayers. "Dear God," he prayed, "I'm not trying to tell you what to do, but could you please send the wind?"

The next day, Johnny walked to the top of the hill. He sat and looked far off at the trees. Suddenly, the sky was dark and birds chirped. Johnny stood up. The trees looked like they were waving—yes! The wind was coming at last!

He felt his hair tickle his skin, and he closed his eyes. The wind blew against his face. He was cool and happy as it tugged at his jeans and flapped his shirt. Then he felt one drop, two, and three. "It's raining!" Johnny shouted, jumping up and down. "Thank you, God! You sent the wind to get the rain!"

The rain fell harder and harder as Johnny ran laughing down the hill.

"You're soaking wet!" his mother said.

Johnny put on dry clothes and stood at the window watching.

His father said, "The weatherman said there would be rain."

"Thank goodness," his mother said, "we needed it."

Johnny didn't say anything. He stood quietly by the window. He knew God had answered his prayers and sent the wind back. It had brought rain. It made the trees dance again. The wind whistled around the windows, and tomorrow it would be waiting for him at the top of the hill.

Mr. Grumble and the Missing Smile

Gloria A. Truitt

Mr. Grumble lived in a big, green house on the corner. He lived all alone except for Molly, his striped cat. Mr. Grumble was old and *very* grumbly and didn't like to be bothered by children. He thought children were noisy, pesty bags of wind.

Poor Mr. Grumble. The only friend he had was Molly. Every afternoon they sat on the front porch, rocking back and forth in Mr. Grumble's creaky, squeaky rocking chair. Mr. Grumble always held Molly on his lap, gently stroking her gray stripes. But Mr. Grumble

never smiled, not even when he was petting Molly. Mr. Grumble didn't know how to smile!

When the neighborhood children walked by, Mr. Grumble would grumble from his porch, "Go away, you noisy, pesty children!" Then all the children would run as fast as they could. All except Laura. She'd smile and say, "Good afternoon, Mr. Grumble." And Mr. Grumble never failed to answer with a *grumble, grumble, grumble.* Poor Mr. Grumble, thought Laura, he must be very unhappy because he *never* smiles.

One day when Laura and her friends John and Peter were passing Mr. Grumble's house, Laura didn't see Mr. Grumble sitting in his creaky, squeaky rocking chair.

"That's strange," said Laura. "Every afternoon he sits on his porch with Molly. I wonder where he is today."

"Never mind," said Peter and John. "By the time we walk back from the park, he'll be there, just waiting to *grumble* at us."

But Mr. Grumble was not sitting on his porch when the children walked back from the park.

"Look! There he is," said Peter. "He's poking around in the bushes—over there." Peter pointed to Mr. Grumble's backyard. Sure enough, Mr. Grumble was searching through the prickly bushes and grumbling more than ever!

John said, "Let's not worry about Mr. Grumble. Besides, we'll be late for dinner if we don't hurry home."

Laura wasn't thinking about dinner. She was thinking about Mr. Grumble. Yet Laura knew that John was right. If she was late, her mother would be worried. The children skipped down the street, forgetting Mr. Grumble.

The next day when the children walked by Mr. Grumble's house, he wasn't sitting on his porch. He was slowly walking *around* it, and his grumbling sounded louder than the day before.

Laura said, "Let's ask him what's wrong. Mr. Grumble never grumbles *that* loudly!"

Peter and John followed Laura across Mr. Grumble's front yard. When Mr. Grumble looked up and saw the children, he frowned and grumbled, "What are you pesty children doing in my yard?"

Laura said, "Good afternoon, Mr. Grumble. Why aren't you sitting in your rocking chair with your cat, Molly? Why do you look so worried?"

"Well," said Mr. Grumble, "I guess I can tell you. I'm worried because I've lost Molly. I haven't seen her since yesterday morning. Now go away and don't bother me!"

"Oh, I'm sorry," said Laura. "I hope you'll find her soon." Laura smiled and waved good-bye to Mr. Grumble, but he didn't smile or wave back. He just stood there, looking very sad.

As the children walked away, Laura said, "I wonder if we could help Mr. Grumble find Molly."

"But where would we look?" asked John. "If Mr. Grumble can't find her, how can we?"

Peter thought for a moment. "Hmmm, I know!" he said. "Mr. Grumble has only been looking *outside* of places. Let's look *inside* of places. Maybe Molly went into a garage or shed and can't get out."

"That's a great idea," said Laura. "Let's hurry!"

The children ran through the neighbors' yards, looking under porches and peeking into trash cans. They looked through garage windows and high up into trees, but could not find Molly anywhere.

"I feel sad," said Laura. "Mr. Grumble has lost his only friend. I can't think of any place we've not looked. What should we do now?"

"Let's go to the park and play," said Peter.

John said, "We might as well. I don't think we'll ever find Molly."

When they arrived at the park, the boys ran to the swings to play. But Laura just sat on the ground thinking. *Where could Molly be?*

After a while, Laura decided to jump rope. Maybe that would make her feel happier. She walked sadly over to the park shed to get the rope. When she opened the door, she couldn't believe her eyes! Right in the middle of the floor sat Molly! She seemed frightened and hungry, so Laura picked her up gently. Molly didn't scratch or try to jump away because she knew that Laura had come to help her. As Laura stepped out of the shed, she called to the boys, "Look what I've found! Molly was locked inside the shed and couldn't get out!"

John and Peter jumped from the swings and ran toward Laura yelling, "Hooray! Let's hurry and show Mr. Grumble what we've found!"

The children ran as fast as they could to Mr. Grumble's house. Laura couldn't run as fast as the boys because she didn't want to shake and frighten Molly.

Mr. Grumble saw the boys running down his driveway and was just getting ready to grumble when Laura came around the corner of the house. As she started down the driveway, Laura called, "Mr. Grumble! Look what we've found!"

Mr. Grumble looked up the driveway and then ran to meet Laura. He gently took Molly in his arms and hugged her. He said, "I want to thank you for finding Molly. You've made me very happy."

The children told him where they had found Molly, then turned and started to leave Mr. Grumble's yard. Suddenly they were surprised to hear Mr. Grumble saying, "I hope you'll come to visit us. Anytime."

As the children turned back to thank Mr. Grumble, they saw the most surprising thing of all. *Mr. Grumble had learned to smile!*

Carlos Sees God's Fireworks

Elizabeth Friedrich

A yellow flash of lightning flew across the sky. *Crash! Roar! Cr-r-runch!* Carlos heard the thunder shake the air. "Daddy, Daddy!" he cried as he dived under his bed.

"Carlos! What's wrong?" His father hurried into the room.

"I'm scared of that loud noise. I don't like it," Carlos said.

"Come out from under your bed now," said his father. "There's something I want to show you." He held out his arms, and Carlos gladly jumped into them. Carlos felt lots better now that his father was holding him.

They walked together into the living room and stood by the screen door. The rain was pounding on the sidewalk. Suddenly another yellow flash flew by. Carlos grabbed his father's leg and closed his eyes. *Crash! Roar! Cr-r-runch!*

"That's what I wanted to show you— God's fireworks," said his father. "The lightning and thunder are the prettiest fireworks I've ever seen. God makes them."

Carlos opened his eyes just a little— in time to see several streaks of gold zoom across the sky. "They *are* pretty, Daddy! But why do they have to make so much noise?"

"God lets us both see and hear his fireworks. They're one of his special gifts to us. And he'll hold us in his arms while we're watching his fireworks—just like I held you before, when you were afraid."

The rain had almost stopped now, and the fireworks were over. "Look over there, Carlos! There's another one of God's special gifts to us."

"Yes," shouted Carlos, "I *like* God's sunbow."

"It's called a rainbow, Carlos."

"But I want to call it a sunbow today because of all the colors sunshining through," Carlos called as he pushed open the screen door. "And because it means that the sun is out, and now I can go outside and play in all the puddles."

A Good Feeling

Verna Sherman

Karla picked up her books and started to the coat room. She didn't even want to come back to school tomorrow. Mrs. Weston, her teacher, had been rushed to the hospital. An *emergency appendectomy* is what Mr. Mills, the principal, had written on the chalkboard.

Karla couldn't even say it. But they were supposed to copy it on a sheet of paper so their parents would know. "And tomorrow," Mr. Mills said, "you'll have a substitute teacher."

But Karla knew no one would be the same as Mrs. Weston. Mrs. Weston was the best teacher she ever had.

She put on her coat and started for home. "Hi, Karla," someone said.

"Hi, Debbie," Karla said to the girl who lived next door.

"What's the matter with you? Have you lost your best friend?" Debbie asked.

"Just about. Mrs. Weston is in the hospital. She's never been sick before. We're going to have a substitute tomorrow."

"Maybe you'll get Candace. She's my brother's girlfriend. She's neat," Debbie said. Then she frowned.

"What's the matter?"

"I forgot. She's teaching somewhere else tomorrow. You'll probably get someone nice—unless you get Mrs. Hake. Everyone calls her Mrs. Hate."

When Karla got home, she had already decided she wouldn't help the new teacher the way she always helped Mrs. Weston. "I'll do the best I can with my schoolwork," she told her family at dinner, "but I won't clean the boards for her like I did for Mrs. Weston. Especially if it's Mrs. Hake."

"The Bible says to 'trust in the Lord and do good,'" her mother said.

"I know, Mom. I do trust the Lord. But I don't trust a new teacher, that's all."

The next morning Karla was up at the usual time. She left for school at the usual time too, but today she walked very slowly.

"Hey, Karla," Mike said, "Mrs. Hake is our teacher."

"Oh, no!" Karla moaned.

Then Mike smiled. "No, she isn't. I was just kidding. I don't know who it is. Maybe it's a man."

"I don't care, I'm not going to help anyone anyway," Karla said, walking into the coat room.

"Good morning. I'm Miss Wilson," a soft voice said behind her. "I'm taking Mrs. Weston's place. What's your name? I have a name badge for you. I don't want to forget any of your names."

Karla looked up into two of the bluest eyes she had ever seen, the same color as the blue in Miss Wilson's blouse. "My name is Karla," she said.

"This is my first day of teaching here at Jefferson. I hope all of you boys and girls will help me a lot," she said. Then she smiled.

Karla couldn't help smiling back.

"I'll show you where the pencil sharpener is," she said. "And the art supplies are over there."

When Karla got home that night, she told her mother all about Miss Wilson. "I feel like she's my friend. Just like Mrs. Weston. And I think she'll understand even if I make mistakes in math, like I usually do. But besides all that, it feels good to do good."

Stolen Treasure

Lois Kaufmann

Billy finished counting his money and looked at his puppy. "Look, Pal, I have almost enough to pay my share of the new bike. Dad said he'd pay the rest." Carefully he put his money back into his treasure box with his arrowheads and agates. He was putting the box back into his secret hiding place in the hollow trunk near the roots of a maple tree when he heard the gate clang.

"Hi, Billy, what are you hiding?"

"Nothing much," Billy answered as his new neighbor, Phil, came running up.

"I saw you put a box in there," Phil said. "Let me see it."

"OK," Billy said, "but don't you dare tell anybody about it." Slowly he drew out the little wooden box.

"Hurry," Phil said. "The other boys are at the vacant lot waiting for us to play ball with them this afternoon."

"I can't. I have to clean out Pal's

house and put clean straw in it."

"I'll help you when the game is over," Phil said, then added, "Wow! Where did you get those arrowheads?"

"My uncle sent them to me from Oklahoma," Billy answered.

"They're just what I need for my Indian collection," Phil said. "I think I'll come and snitch them sometime when you aren't looking. Now let's hurry and play ball."

Billy stuck his treasures back into the secret hiding place. "Now I'll have to find a new hiding place, and I'll never find such a good one as this," he grumbled to himself.

Billy grabbed his glove and called in the door. "Mom, Phil said if I play ball a while, he'll help me clean Pal's house later. OK?"

"You'll have to do it before supper," she answered. "Tonight is junior chorus practice."

"OK," Billy said and whistled for Pal.

"Leave Pal at home," Phil said. "He's a nuisance on the ball field."

"Sorry, Pal," Billy told his dog. "You'll have to stay home this time." Quickly he closed the gate and turned his back on his yapping puppy.

The ball game was exciting, and no one bothered to think about the time until Phil's little sister came and called him for supper.

"Supper!" Billy exclaimed. "I was supposed to clean Pal's house before supper!"

"I'll help you in the morning," puffed Phil as they ran toward home.

When Billy came home, his family was ready for supper. He took a swipe at his hands and face as he passed the sink. Then he dropped breathlessly into his chair.

"Made it!" Dad grinned as he remembered the times he had made the same dash home for meals.

"Phil said he'd help me first thing in the morning," Billy said in answer to his mother's questioning look.

Next morning Billy was up early. He gobbled down his breakfast, picked up his weekly allowance, and hurried out to get his treasure chest from its secret hiding place. He reached for his treasure box and let out a yell. "Pal! My treasure is gone!" He dug wildly around in the space under the tree. "That Phil! He said he was going to steal my arrowheads. The old thief!"

"What's all the noise about?" his mother asked, coming to the door.

"Phil stole my money and my treasures," Billy cried.

"You kept your money out here?" she asked in surprise.

"Uh-huh," said Billy, wiping his eyes. "I had a hidden treasure chest like you read about in stories. Now Phil stole it."

"What makes you think Phil took it?" his mother wanted to know.

"Nobody else knew about it. Just yesterday he said he was going to steal my arrowheads."

"That doesn't prove he took them," she said. "Let me look." Just then the telephone rang. As soon as his mother was safely in the house, Billy ran out the gate.

"I'm going to get my treasure back from that old stealer," he said. Then he saw Phil running toward him.

"Hi, Billy," Phil called. "Are you ready to clean Pal's house?"

"You get out of here, you old thief,

and don't you ever come back!" Billy shouted.

"Wh-what?" Phil gasped, skidding to a stop.

"My treasures are gone, and you took them!" Billy said.

"I did not!" Phil answered hotly. "I never touched your old junk!" He turned home, stomping as he went.

Slowly Billy went back to his empty treasure hole. Pal ran in and sniffed around. "Come, Pal, I'll work on your house until Mom comes out." He kicked angrily at a stone in his path.

He started pulling dirty straw out of Pal's house. Just as he reached in the second time, something shiny caught his eye. There was a quarter in the straw, and a dime. Then he saw part of a dollar bill. He reached in and pulled out his chewed-up treasure box. He sat back on his heels and squirmed as he remembered how he had accused Phil a few minutes before.

Slowly Billy got up and started for Phil's house. Phil was hitting angrily at a fence post with his bat. He glared at Billy.

"I'm sorry, Phil," Billy said in a low voice. "Pal was the thief. He took my treasure box to his house and chewed it up."

"So?" Phil asked.

"So—please forgive me," Billy said, "I'm sorry."

Slowly the angry look left Phil's face. He smiled.

"OK," he said. "I'll forgive you *this* time, but—"

"But don't let it happen again!" broke in Billy. They laughed and started toward Billy's house to clean up the mess.

Move Along
Ron Matthies

George Henry said, "Good-bye, Craig." Craig didn't look at him. Tubby said, "Good-bye," and Craig heard his nose snuffle a tiny bit. He didn't look at Tubby either. He did mumble, "Good-bye," but he didn't look; he couldn't look because he knew more than his nose would snuffle. It was the same when Legs and Freckles and the others said good-bye. He didn't look. He just mumbled.

Then he rolled up the car window and sank into the cushions. He heard the guys shouting behind the car as it turned from the drive and hummed down the street. Soon they were beyond the voices and the sight of his home, which stood empty and gathering dust while his family left it—deserted it—to move 150 miles away to a new house, not a new home. It would never be home, he thought.

For what seemed like the three-millionth time, he leaned toward the front seat and said, "Why do we have to move, Dad?" He father shrugged a quick look back at him and said, "You know my company transferred me, Craig. I either go to Lakeville or stay in Alfreesboro and find a new job."

Craig humped back into the cushions and said, "Oh." That's all Craig said, but not all he thought. Dad should have found another job. How could he do this? How could he make me leave George Henry and Tubby and everyone to move to some nowhere town?

His mother stretched her hand into the back seat and took his hand. She said softly, gently, "You'll like Lakeville, Craig. You'll make new friends."

He jerked his hand from hers. "Never. Not like the old friends."

She smiled and said, "I hope they're not exactly like the old ones. It would be dull if God made everyone exactly alike."

"It wouldn't bother me."

His father whirled around a curve, then said, "Well, Craig, he does make people the same in some ways. Everyone is anxious to make new friends."

"I'm not," he said.

So the rest of the trip was quiet. They didn't talk to him. He stared out the window without seeing the hills or the lakes or the trees. He just saw his old home. He just saw the gang running up the hill and playing ball in the meadow. When they slowed down for Lakeville, population 3,129, he still stared out the window and saw Alfreesboro, population 18,412. When they stopped at their new house, he still saw their old one.

But he didn't say anything more about his feelings. His mother was too excited about shoving furniture into new corners. His father was too busy screwing curtain rods into place and tacking up picture hangers. They scarcely noticed him until it was bedtime and he climbed into his bunk between the unpacked boxes and newspaper-covered windows. Then they noticed him because, when he prayed and they listened, he said, "God bless George Henry and Tubby and Legs and the hill and all my friends."

He didn't mention them or their new house. They shook their heads and didn't say anything except, "Goodnight, Craig. Sleep well."

During the next few days, as he watched from the porch, he saw boys running across backyards and heading for a big open lot. They played ball there. At least they do that the same, he thought. But he didn't leave the porch. He didn't walk to the lot himself. He stayed home and growled most of the time and said, "Who wants these farmers for friends?"

That's what he said and did until one day when, as he stood on the porch, he heard a door slam next door. He heard feet pounding on the hard ground. They came closer to him, closer and closer, until the feet had legs and arms

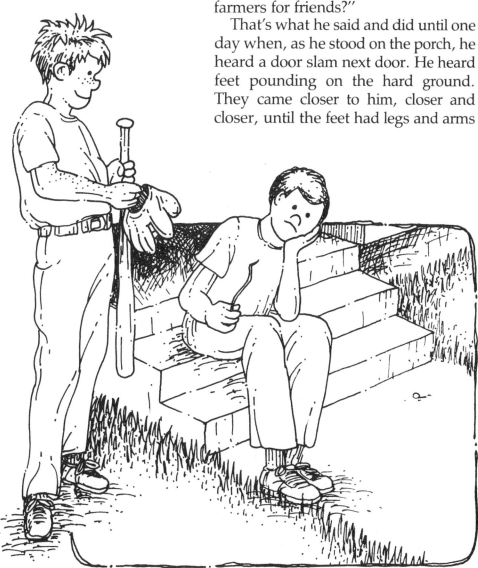

and a head. Craig stared at the big round face and the red hair. It stuck out in every direction. The mouth said, "I'm Harvey. My friends call me Red."

Craig mumbled, "I see why."

Red smiled and shoved fingers through the hair. He said, "You want to go to the field and play ball?"

Craig said, "I guess not."

Red said, "Oh, come on. You'll like the other guys."

"Maybe I'll come for a little while," he said. But I'm not playing long, he thought. I won't make friends with these guys.

That's what he thought, but when suppertime came, he hurried through the shadows with Red and Floyd and John. He pounded Floyd on the back when they came to his house and said, "See you tomorrow." He smiled when John dropped off for his house and said, "I'll come over tomorrow and look at your train." Then he and Red were at their yards. He said, "Thanks for asking me to play."

Red said, "Sure. Everyone wants new friends."

He said, "I guess you're right."

At supper he smiled and his parents asked, "Are you happy?"

He said, "Yes. You were right. I guess it's lucky God doesn't make everyone the same. It's fun to know different people. You were right, too, about everyone needing friends."

When he went to bed, he prayed, "God bless Red and Floyd and John, and God bless our new home."

That's what he prayed, and then he added sleepily, "God bless George Henry and Tubby and Legs too."

The Broken Window Elizabeth Wedge

Mom, do you know what? Today a boy in my room was almost late for school. He came running in fast and slammed the door. And do you know what happened then? The window in the door broke into a million pieces!"

"Well, that's too bad, David. He should have been more careful," his mother said absentmindedly. Then she added, "Go wash for dinner and comb your hair." David really wanted to talk a little more about the broken window, but right then didn't seem to be the time for it. They were going to Grandpa and Grandma's house that evening, and David was going to spend the night. So David forgot all about the broken window.

Grandpa was funny. He made up funny little poems or changed old ones and made you laugh and laugh. When he said "Old Mother Hubbard," he didn't say it the way other people did. He said:

Old Mother Hubbard
Went to the cupboard
To get her poor dog a bone.
When she got there
The cupboard was bare
And so the poor dog had to eat oatmeal!

David could hardly wait to get to Grandpa and Grandma's house, and the evening went so fast he didn't even think of the broken window again until Grandma was tucking him in bed and listening to his prayers. He wanted to tell Grandma all about it. But when he started, "Grandma, do you know what?" she said, "Hush, David, it's late and you must get to sleep or I won't be able to get you up in time for school."

When David went to school the next morning, the window was all fixed! He was glad he hadn't told anyone. Mom hadn't seemed to be too concerned anyway. She didn't even ask if the little boy got hurt. What was that Miss Brown was saying? "Children, Mr. Toms put the new window in for us this morning, but in order to help us all learn to take better care of our school, I'm asking each of you to bring a quarter to school tomorrow to help pay for it." Now what'd she have to go do that for?

"Mom, you know that window that got broken that I told you about? Well, Miss Brown wants each one in the room to bring a quarter to help pay for it."

"I don't think that's right," his mother said. "I think the parents of the child that did it should pay for it." Just then the telephone rang, and she went to answer it.

The next morning his mother didn't give him the money or say anything about it. He went off to school, but he didn't skip on the way or whistle. He wasn't feeling very happy. When the other children turned in their quarters, what would he say? That he'd forgotten? But he hadn't. He'd just have to tell the truth—his mother wouldn't let him bring it.

Miss Brown didn't ask him if he had brought his money, but she did ask him to pass an envelope around the room for all the children to put their quarters in. Would anyone notice that he didn't put any money in it? No one said anything. They didn't notice! He tried not to think about it, but it bothered him.

He was almost glad the night that his mother came home from PTA and he overheard her say to his dad, "I was never so embarrassed in my whole life! Do you know who broke that window that I refused to send a quarter to help pay for? It was our David!"

Daddy said, "I wonder why he didn't tell us?"

David could have pretended to be asleep, but he wanted so much to feel happy again. He climbed out of bed, went out to the living room, and stood in the doorway with his head bowed, his face red, and his eyes full of tears.

"I meant to tell you. I really did. I didn't mean to break that window, and I didn't mean to lie to you either. I didn't lie to you with words, did I, Mom? But I guess not all lying is with words."

He began to cry. Mother put her arms around him and drew him up onto her lap. "I'm sorry too," she said. "I should have listened when you wanted to talk to me. I think we've both made a mistake. Now we'll just have to forgive each other and try not to let such a thing happen again."

David put his arms around her neck and kissed her. She was the most wonderful mother in the whole world!

He had already said his prayers, but when he went back to bed he found himself talking to God again:

"Thank you, God, for my mother. Thank you, God, that she's not mad at me. I'm sorry for the way I acted." He snuggled happily down in the covers. "Goodnight, God, I love you. Amen." Soon he was fast asleep.

God Is Always Near

Mabel N. McCaw

The moon shines in my window
when I go to bed at night;
it makes a silver pathway
with its cheery light.

I think that it is saying
in its own quiet way
that God is always near me
in nighttime or in day.

Love One Another

Helen Kronberg

Jane and her father sat side by side on the davenport as Jane read her Sunday school story aloud. Jane was in the second grade now and could read almost all of the words without any help.

"That's very good, Jane," her father said. "Let's see if you remember the Bible verse."

"Sure, that's easy," Jane answered. "Love one another."

Her father nodded and smiled.

"Andy should go to Sunday school so he can learn 'Love one another,'" Jane said.

"Who is Andy?" her father asked.

"A new kid at school. He is the worst kid I ever saw."

"Why? What does he do?" her father asked.

"He hits kids all the time. He grabs their papers. He hits their arms and makes them scribble when they are trying to write. He even swears sometimes."

"Maybe he's lonely and scared in a new school. Maybe if you would all be extra nice to him, he would be nicer too," her father replied.

"Be nice to him! Dad, he's awful!" Jane wailed.

"God says to love one another," her father reminded her.

"Who could love Andy?"

"Just think about it a little," her father told her. He left Jane and went into the kitchen.

Jane pondered the question. It didn't seem right that God could expect her to love anyone like Andy. How could even God love someone who acted like Andy did? But God loves everyone, she reminded herself.

The other children came in from play, and Jane forgot about Andy until she was getting ready for bed.

When she said her prayers that night, she asked God to help her. "God bless Andy," she prayed. "I don't like him, God. But if you say I should, I'll try to love him anyway."

The next morning she almost wished Andy would not be at school when she got there. She had promised God that she would try to love him, but she didn't see

how she could keep that promise.

Sure enough, there he was, teasing the children on the playground. Jane started up the walk, and he raced across the yard. He knocked her book out of her hands.

Tears sprang to Jane's eyes. She quickly stooped to pick up the book. She swallowed hard to keep back her anger and walked on toward the door.

There was a scuffle near the monkey bars. The teacher firmly took Andy by the arm and marched him inside. The other boy was comforted by his playmates.

Later, while Andy's reading group was in class, Jane listened as he stumbled over the words. He really is dumb, she thought. I could read that story last year, when I was only in first grade.

The teacher shook her head sadly. "Andy, you are going to need a great deal of help. We cannot go on like this," she said. She looked at the children who were still at their desks. "You children have all had this story. I need someone to help Andy with his reading. Who would like to do that?" she asked.

No one raised a hand.

Jane remembered her father's words. "Maybe he is scared and lonely," he had said.

Jane raised her hand. "I'll help him," she said.

The teacher nodded her approval. "Good!" she said. "Andy, go with Jane to that corner table. With extra help, I'm sure you will soon catch up to the other children in your group. Let's try!"

Andy shuffled over to the table and slumped into a chair. "Who cares about school anyway? Maybe we will move soon and I won't have to go to school any more."

"Not go to school!" Jane whispered. "You have to go to school! How can you ever learn if you don't go to school?"

Andy shrugged. "Lots of times I don't go to school. Sometimes there are no schools where we live."

Jane could not understand how there could be a place with no schools. But she knew he was telling the truth. She also knew that he was only pretending that he did not care.

The teacher tapped on her desk. "Read, don't talk," she told them.

Jane smiled at Andy. "We'd better get busy. Don't be scared. I didn't know all the words at first either. I had to practice."

"You did?" Andy asked in surprise.

Jane nodded. He opened the book and began to read.

The Boy Who Liked God
Ron Matthies

Billy liked God. He liked the way God made the sun shine on puddles after a rainstorm. He liked the trees that folded their tops and bent in the wind. God wasn't like Billy's other friends who tossed balls and pretended war and then had to go home to supper. God was always there. He never left for anything.

Billy's favorite place to play was in the meadow. It was off by itself where you couldn't see any houses. It was just this big, open place on a hill with tall, brown grass and a big tree with branches hanging almost to the ground. Billy could run up the hill until he was out of breath, then lie down on the grass and let it tickle his face and arms. Or he could climb the tree and sit there with the leaves all humped over him, hiding him from everything.

Here, on this highest hill around, Billy thought he must be closer to his friend God than any place else. Here on the hill he could probably even see God. So Billy would squint his eyes into tiny slits and peek at the sun. He could see all different colors—purple and orange, red and blue. Then his eyes would hurt from the brightness, and he would have to look away. But Billy knew that if the sun weren't so bright, he could see God and God would walk with him and lie in the grass and climb the tree.

Billy didn't mind that he couldn't see God—he knew he was there. So every day Billy came to his hill and ran through the brown of the grass and laughed when he heard the birds sing and saw the sun on the leaves of his tree. Often it all made Billy so happy that he would look up, smile, and say, "Hi, God." And he knew God heard and understood.

One day when Billy was playing on the hill, he heard a sound like one of those toy animals that squeaks when you squeeze it. He looked all through the grass and finally found the noise. It was a bird, a bird with a broken wing. Billy held his breath. It was the most beautiful bird he had ever seen. He carefully reached into the grass and touched the bird. He could feel its feathers ruffling and bending as his fingers touched them. Then he picked it up and said, "Hi, bird." He held his arms way out with the bird in his hand, almost as if it were in the sky.

The sun shone on the blue feathers and made gold spots all over the bird. Billy laughed and the bird began to sing.

Billy just stood there with the bluebird in his hands and listened to it sing. Then, because the bird was so beautiful and sang such a pretty song, Billy hugged the bird to himself and said, "Oh, hi, bird. Hi, bird with the broken wing."

But when he quit hugging the bird, it didn't sing anymore and it didn't move. Billy said, "Sing, bird! Sing! Oh, please sing," but it didn't.

Billy ran up and down the meadow shouting, "I killed it. I squeezed it too hard. I just hugged it to show how much I liked it. Oh, God, I'm sorry. I'm sorry." He stopped running and stood there. God didn't hear me, he thought. God isn't my friend anymore because I killed his bird. I killed God's bird and now he isn't my friend.

When Billy had buried the bird, he walked slowly down the hill and didn't look back. He never went back to his hill or looked in the sky and he never said, "Hi, God," any more. He just played with his other friends, his friends who didn't know what he had done to the bird. He didn't laugh as much or sing as much or even run as often. He never told anyone, not even his mom or dad, what he had done.

Then one Sunday he was sitting in church. He squirmed and kept thinking he shouldn't be in God's house when God wasn't his friend any more.

Suddenly he sat up and listened. Pastor Brown was saying, "Because of Jesus, all people, no matter how wrong

their deeds, can be forgiven." That's all Billy heard, but he wondered, wondered if this meant him too.

He waited after the service, and, when everyone had left, he tugged at Pastor Brown's robe and said, "May I talk to you?"

Pastor Brown said, "Certainly, Bill."

"You know today when you were talking about forgiveness and all that, did that mean that if I did something really, really awful, and as soon as I did it I was sorry, does that mean that God says, 'OK, Billy. I still like you'?"

"That's what it means, Bill."

Billy said, "No matter how terrible? Even if I killed something and was sorry, he'd say, 'OK, Billy'?"

"Yes, Bill."

Billy ran out of the church shouting, "Thanks, Pastor. Thanks a lot." He was on the sidewalk and could hear his good shoes clicking on the cement. Then he was off the cement and could just hear his shoes scraping on the gravel and stone. He began to run, run as fast as he could up his hill. When he got to the top, he was out of breath.

Billy looked around. He looked a long time at the hill. He saw the tree was still there, and the grass. The sun was shining the same as he remembered. He smiled, looked into the sky, and said, "Hi, God! Oh, hi, God!"

David and the Jellyfish

Sue Guist

When David turned out the bedroom light, his brother, Billy, started to cry. "Come on, Billy, don't be a crybaby," David scolded. "Swimming lessons start tomorrow. I need my sleep."

"I can't sleep in the dark," little Billy sobbed. "I'm afraid."

David pulled his head under the covers so he couldn't hear Billy. He had his own troubles. Vacation was coming. He couldn't go out in a boat with Dad till he learned to swim. And he was afraid of water.

When David got to the pool next morning, the others there were splashing and frolicking like a school of happy porpoises. He wondered whether to climb down the ladder or jump in all at once. Just then a whistle blew. He took a deep breath, closed his eyes, and jumped. Cold water was everywhere.

When his feet touched bottom, David opened his eyes. The water came only halfway up his chest. The whistle blew again. While everyone quieted, the teacher looked them over. "A lively bunch. We'll have you swimming like champs in two weeks."

All but me, David thought.

"First, let's get to know the water." The teacher slapped his hand down in a splash that showered them all. "If you fight it, you can use a lot of energy to get nowhere. If you trust it, water can be your friend. It will even hold you up. Now here's how you make a squirt-bug. Try it."

David clenched his fist under water. With practice, he could squirt a stream a long way. This could be fun. But then someone squirted him right in the eye.

"Hey," David yelled, "don't do that."

"Come on, bet you can't squirt me." He didn't want to squirt anybody. David hated water in his face. He couldn't understand the others. They didn't care how wet they got.

Another whistle ended the squirt-bug game. "Line up," the teacher said. "Now watch this."

To David's horror, the teacher put his head right in the water. He wrapped his arms around his knees and bobbed there, silently, for a long time. At last the teacher put his feet down, shook water out of his ears like a dog, and grinned at them.

"Jellyfish float. Try it. Take a deep breath, put your face in, lift your feet, let go."

The boy next to David came up choking and sputtering. The teacher patted his back. "All right, fellow? Next time take that deep breath before you get to the water." Everybody laughed, except David. He was trying to work up courage to try the jellyfish.

At last the lesson ended. David still hadn't put his face in the water. He was no fish. He didn't belong under water. He had to think of something.

At bedtime that night David bent over the washbowl. Gripping the rim, he lowered his face into the water. He dipped his chin. He dunked his forehead. But he couldn't put his whole face in at once.

"I'll have to quit," he said to the mirror, water dripping from his eyebrows. "I'll have to let Dad down." Another summer of wading by the dock with Billy.

"David, come quick," his brother called. "I'm scared."

David dashed for the bedroom. "What is it?"

His brother pointed to the window. "There's something out there, in the tree. Something awful, David, don't look."

David opened the window. "No, don't," Billy cried. "It'll get you."

David leaned out into the night.

"It's your kite, Billy. Don't you remember? It got stuck in the tree."

"Ohhh." Billy came over to see for himself. "That was silly, to be afraid of my kite. How old do you have to be before you're not afraid of anything?"

"I don't know if anybody gets that old." David climbed into bed. "It's not what you're afraid of, it's what you do

about it that counts. I used to be afraid of the dark, till Mother told me it's friendly. Nighttime lets people and animals rest."

"Mmm." Billy was almost asleep. David wished he could fix his own trouble so easily. But water in his face—he could never get used to that. Or could he? Once he hadn't liked darkness in his face.

The teacher said water is friendly. It will hold you up if you trust it. He could try.

Next day, when his turn came for the jellyfish, David took a deep breath. He put his face in the pool. Cold water felt strange in his ears. He made himself stay. He lifted his feet and brought up his knees.

A wonderful feeling came over David. He bobbed there, not touching anything. The friendly water did hold him up.

David came up sputtering, laughing, and shaking himself. "I can float!"

"I knew you could," the teacher said. "But you had to believe it too. Now, let's learn to swim."

Good-Night, Dear World

Solveig Paulson Russell

Good-night, dear world, it's sleep time now;
the stars blink in the sky,
and breezes in the poplar leaves
are crooning lullaby.

The moon is just a crescent moon,
boat-shaped and sailing high;

and though I cannot see them now
nighttime creatures fly.

The owls, the bats, the moths are out,
they flit as night slips by.
Each one is in its rightful place—
and here too, safe, am I.

A Nickle Bet

Craig Nagel

Robin burst into the kitchen all out of breath and asked, "Mom, how big is God?"

"Bigger than anybody can imagine," replied her mother, who was washing dishes.

"Is he bigger than Dad?" asked Robin. "I bet Suzie that Dad was bigger than God."

"Well, I'm afraid you lost the bet," said her mother, shaking her head. "God is much bigger than Dad."

"Oh, no!" said Robin. "Now I have to pay Suzie a nickel, and I don't have any money."

"Perhaps that will teach you not to make bets," said her mother. "But since you don't have any money, you can work for me. I'll give you a nickel if you'll help me dry the dishes. Then you can pay Suzie the nickel you owe her."

"All right," agreed Robin. She took a bright blue dish towel from the rack and started in on a green glass. When she was finished with the glass, she set it carefully on the table.

Then she picked out a white cup and began drying it. As she worked, she asked her mother some more questions.

"Is God bigger than a car?" she asked.

"Yes, Robin. God is bigger than a car."

"Well, is he bigger than a house?" she asked.

"Yes, dear. God is even bigger than a house," her mother answered.

"That's really big," said Robin as she placed the white cup on the table beside the green glass.

She was just starting on a red bowl when her mother said, "You know, Robin, God is so big that he can fit around the whole world. The Bible speaks of the earth as God's footstool."

Robin frowned. Then she said, "But Mom, if God is that big, my Sunday school

teacher must be wrong."

"What do you mean?" asked her mother. "Why would your Sunday school teacher be wrong?"

"Because," Robin answered, "he told us to let God come into our hearts. And if God's so big that he uses the world for a footrest, then he couldn't possibly fit into our hearts."

"Oh, Robin!" her mother laughed. "I see now why you are asking all these questions." She finished washing the last dish and pulled the stopper in the sink. The water gurgled and hissed as it went down the drain. Then she said, "You see, God *is* bigger than the whole world. But that doesn't mean he can't come into our hearts. God is a spirit, which means he can move anywhere he wants to or fit into any heart that will let him in. In a way, he's like air. Air surrounds the whole world, but it still fits into your body when you breathe it in."

Robin finished drying the red bowl and set it on the table. Then she said, "Well, if God is like air, what does he need a footstool for?"

Her mother squeezed out the dishrag. Then she said, "He doesn't really need a footstool, dear. To say that the earth is God's footstool is simply a way of showing that he is much bigger than anything we can imagine. But the important thing is not how much *space* God would take up if we could see him, but rather that he is big in a different way."

"What way?" Robin frowned.

"In the way of our fears," said her mother. "In the way of our problems. God is bigger than the biggest problem. He is greater than the greatest fear. His love is greater than the greatest hatred."

Robin was silent. She didn't fully understand what her mother was talking about, but she did understand a little. "Well," she said at last, "I guess it takes a lot of thinking to understand about God."

"You're right," said her mother. "And even if we spent the rest of our lives trying to understand God, we still would never know all about him."

Robin hung the dish towel on the rack. "I think it would be worth a try," she said.

Joey's Surprise

Ann Hudson Downs

When Joey heard his mother come into the room, he quickly hid his face in his pillow.

"Good morning, and a happy seventh birthday, Joey!" she called cheerfully.

"What's happy about it?" Joey said.

"I'm sorry, Joey," his mother said softly. "I know how much you wanted to be the birthday boy at school. But Dr. Smith said you should stay in bed one more day just to make sure you are well." Then she gently patted the back of Joey's head.

Just then the telephone rang downstairs and his mother left to answer. Joey heard her say, "Oh, that would be wonderful!" Then she said, "How very kind!" After that Joey didn't feel like listening anymore.

All day Joey kept remembering Sally Mason's birthday last week. Mr. Jensen had taken the birthday hat down from the closet shelf and placed it on Sally's head. It had "Happy Birthday" printed in silver sequins across the front. Then everybody sang the birthday song. All day Sally wore the beautiful hat, and everybody was especially nice to her.

Near the end of the day, Sally's mother had brought a big birthday cake for Mr. Jensen and all the children to share. Joey had fun, but he kept thinking about his own birthday.

Just before it was time to go home, Mr. Jensen had looked at the birthday calendar with all the red circles. "I see we have a date circled for next week," he said. "I wonder whose birthday that can be?"

Joey remembered he had felt a little shy when he raised his hand. The children had looked at him, and they smiled too. But I had to get the flu and spoil it all! he thought. Joey looked at the clock on the wall. He thought it must be about time for the children to be leaving school. He wondered if they had forgotten all about his red circle. Maybe they didn't even miss him or think about his birthday.

Mother came into the room. "Your teacher called," she said.

"Did he remember my birthday?" Joey asked.

His mother smiled. "Look out the window and see."

What Joey saw made his eyes grow big and round. There below his window stood Mr. Jensen and Joey's best friends from school. When they saw him looking out, they began to sing, "Happy birthday, dear Joey. Happy birthday to you!" At the same time Mother was placing the birthday hat on his head.

The next minute Mother was cutting a big cake into many pieces. "For Mr. Jensen and my friends?" Joey asked.

"That's right," his mother answered. "And here's a piece for you."

Joey wasn't very hungry, but it was fun to wear the birthday hat and watch his friends enjoy his birthday cake.

Soon it was time for Joey's friends to say good-bye. The children shouted, "Good-bye, Joey," as Mr. Jensen loaded them into the school station wagon.

Just before he drove away, Mr. Jensen turned and waved. "Many more happy birthdays, Joey," he called.

"Thank you! Thank you!" Joey called back. "But this birthday will always be the best," he said softly. "My friends didn't forget."

Billy's Promise

Kit Lambeth

Billy was too excited to even think of eating breakfast. What fun he would have playing with his friend Toby.

"Toby invited me to stay all day, Mom. Please, may I go?" he asked.

"Toby is a good friend. I know you enjoy playing with him," Mother said softly.

"Toby is my very best friend," Billy said. "We're going to help his grandfather gather his pumpkins today." He put on his thick, woolly sweater and pulled his cap down over his ears.

"Have you forgotten that you promised to play with Marta this afternoon?" asked Mother.

Billy looked down at the floor. He had forgotten!

Marta was Billy's friend from next door. She couldn't see like other children. Her doctors said she would have to start wearing thick glasses. Billy helped her walk to school each day and to the park on Saturday. Sometimes Marta went to Sunday school and church with Billy and his parents.

"I can't break my promise to Marta. She needs me," Billy said thoughtfully. "But I wanted to play with Toby today. He said if I helped harvest the pumpkins, he'd give me one." Billy sat down at the breakfast table again to think.

All at once he clapped his hands together. "I know what I can do," he declared. "I can play awhile with Marta, then I can ask if she could go with us to the farm."

"That's a good idea," Mother replied. "I'll call Toby's mother to see if it's all right for Marta to come. Remember, you'll have to help Marta on the farm."

"Toby and I will help her," Billy promised. "She'll have as much fun as we will."

It wasn't long before Toby and his father came by to take Billy and Marta to the farm.

"I've never seen a farm before," Marta said happily. "I'll see so many new things!"

"How can she see things on a farm?" Toby whispered to Billy. "She can't see to walk to school alone."

"I'll show you when we get to the farm," Billy whispered back. "Marta can see more than you think."

All the way to the farm, Billy and Marta and Toby sang the songs they had learned in school. Soon the pickup truck was bouncing along on a country road.

"We're almost there!" Toby exclaimed.

"Tell me, Billy, what do you see?" asked Marta.

"There are trees, and their leaves are all orange and red and yellow, like your shirt, Marta," Billy explained. "There is a farmhouse, and there are cattle eating grass in the field. There is a man driving a red tractor. There is a wagon behind the tractor and it's filled with big, yellow balls."

"Those yellow balls must be pumpkins. We're at Toby's grandfather's farm!" Marta shouted.

"Say, you're right," said Toby's father. He turned into the driveway, and Toby and Billy helped Marta out.

"What do you see now, Billy?" asked Marta.

"There are shocks of corn in the garden and ducks floating on the pond where the cattle drink," said Billy. Then he took Marta's hands and put something soft and furry in them.

Marta held it close to her ear. "It's a kitten!" she said, laughing. "I love baby kittens. What color is it, Billy?"

Just then Toby winked at Billy. "Let me tell her," he whispered.

"It's as white as snow," Toby began, "and its eyes are like little blue marbles. Its tongue is pink and its ears are tiny."

"I like your grandfather's farm, Toby," said Marta.

Toby looked surprised. "How did you know it was me talking?" he asked, puzzled.

"I listen more carefully now that I can't see so well," Marta answered. "I learn a lot by listening. And I have Billy to help me."

Billy smiled. "Now you know how Marta can see so many things on a farm, Toby."

"Yes," said Toby. "You help her see."

"And Marta helps me hear things that I've never heard before," Billy replied.

"What can she hear that you can't?" Toby asked.

"She can hear squirrels playing in the trees and crickets moving in the grass," said Billy.

"God gives us friends to help," Toby's father said gently.

"He gives us friends who help us too," Billy added. "I'm glad I kept my promise to Marta. This way, we've all had fun."

Autumn Sigh

Craig Nagel

Timmy Jenkins gulped down the last of his milk, wiped his face with a big, candy-striped napkin, and sighed. It was getting colder in the evenings these days, and the days were growing shorter. It was autumn, and something about autumn made Timmy Jenkins feel like sighing.

"Do you want dessert?" asked his mother as she reached for her cup of coffee.

"Hmmm? Oh, no. No, thank you," said Timmy. Then he sighed again, a long, sad sigh, and folded his candy-striped napkin.

His mother looked at him. She was frowning, and Timmy knew she was puzzled. "What's the matter, Mom?" he asked.

"That's just what I was going to ask," said his mother. "What's the matter with you? You sit there and stare out the window and sigh, and you seem so sad. What's wrong?"

Timmy was silent. He looked out the window. A dead leaf see-sawed on the air as it sank toward the ground. The evening shadows were longer now and darker, and in the distance Timmy heard a mourning dove cry.

"I don't know," he said at last. "I don't know what makes me feel so sad, but I can't help it."

His mother took a sip of coffee. Then she said, "Well, perhaps it's because of the weather. Autumn always makes me feel a little sad too."

Timmy didn't say anything. He simply stared out the window at the falling leaves and the creeping shadows and sighed. Later his mother asked him if he wanted to take a walk. Timmy agreed, and soon they were outside walking down the street.

Timmy sniffed the air. Someone was burning leaves, and the smell of leaf smoke burned in his nose and made the air seem dark and heavy. Autumn, he thought. Why does autumn have to come? Autumn means death and smoke and sadness. He sighed again.

"Look!" his mother pointed toward the sky. Through the trees Timmy saw a long, wavering V-shape. The geese were flying south for the winter. Why? Timmy wondered. Why do the birds have to leave? Just because it gets a little chilly, everything either turns brown and dies or else flies away. Why? He felt angry at the thought of leaves dying and birds flying away.

"I hate autumn," he said out loud.

"What?"

"I said I hate autumn," said Timmy. "I hate the smell of burnt leaves and the color of dead leaves and the geese having to fly away. It seems like the whole world is going to die."

He kicked at a stone in the road. Then he sighed again.

"I'm afraid you're forgetting something," said Timmy's mother.

"What?" said Timmy. "What am I forgetting?"

"You're forgetting how you felt in spring," said his mother. "You're forgetting how excited you were when you saw the first robin returning and how good the green trees looked after seeing white snow for so long."

Timmy closed his eyes. He thought about spring and how wonderful it had been to run around without a heavy winter coat and to watch the first green spears of grass push up out of the earth. Then he thought about autumn and the dying leaves and the chilly evenings. It did seem to make a little bit of sense, this coming and going of birds and the growing and dying of leaves.

"It's all part of a plan," said his mother. "Without death there could be no birth, and without going away there could be no returning."

Timmy opened his eyes. The air still seemed dark and heavy. The faraway cry of the mourning dove seemed sadder than before. He looked up at the sky. The geese had shrunk to the size of pencil points.

He knew his mother was right. Without autumn there could be no spring. Without sadness there could be no joy.

A dead leaf twisted to the ground before him. Timmy sighed. Then he smiled. And then he sighed again.

One of Those Days

Ron Matthies

George Henry snapped up. The blankets plopped around his middle. When he climbed out of his pajamas, they hung around his ankles, so he kicked them off. He could tell already that it was one of those days. His mother would say he got up on the wrong side of the bed, but this time he'd fool her. He climbed into bed and out the other side. Now he'd gotten up on both sides of the bed. It didn't help. It was still one of those days.

At breakfast he squinted at his plate and said, "Yuck. Eggs again. Is that all you can cook?"

His mother said, "They're good for you."

When he finished the eggs, even scraping the last yellow piece of the yolk from his plate, he stalked to the window. It was a nice day. He hated to admit it, but it was nice. The lilacs were purpling everywhere, and the smell even came in through the window. The clotheslines clattered in the wind like tiny drums, and the birds made such a noise that he hardly heard his mother sneak up behind him and throw her arms around his chest to hug him. She said, "The lilacs sure smell good, don't they?"

George Henry answered, "They're too sweet. They smell like maple syrup." He tugged away from her, almost ripping his yellow T-shirt, and ran up the stairs to find his crayons. He always colored on his bad days. If he colored hard enough, he might hear the Prussian blue or the Naples yellow go Snap! and break. He was careful to use colors he didn't like much because he wouldn't want to break a pretty green or red that he might need on a good day. He colored for a long time, but no crayons broke, so he took a big swipe at the page. The crayon slid, squeaked across the page, bumped down the sides, and made a big burnt sienna loop right on the linoleum of his floor. "Oops," he said, but he didn't really mean it. He only said it because he thought someone might have seen him.

By lunchtime he didn't feel any better, even though he'd taken his crane apart and hid a screw so his father couldn't fix it. His mother handed him his plate. Sitting right in the middle, staring up at him, was a tuna fish sandwich.

He banged his elbows on the table, fit his hands around the red of his hair, and said, "I hate tuna fish. I won't eat it."

His mother said, "It's good for you."

He said, "The way you feed me, I'll be the healthiest kid on the block. I still won't eat it."

His mother knit her arms together and shifted her hip. The stripes of her dress went sideways, blue then green. She mumbled, "You certainly do know how to make it hard to love you sometimes."

He said, "Then don't bother."

She said, "Unless you shape up, I won't bother."

George Henry skidded the plate across the table. It hung for a second on the edge, then went Crash! The tuna fish and the plate were all over the floor.

His mother grabbed his arm, her brown hair hanging almost in his face. "George Henry Amadeus Lawson, you are the most hateful boy. I just scrubbed the floor. Now go to your room and stay there."

He went to his room, but he didn't stay there. He crept to the bathroom and filled his canteen, then waited for his mother to go outside before he sneaked down the steps. He climbed up the stool and took the top off the fat bear cookie jar. He filled his bag with cookies and olives and cake, then threw in a bottle of Coke and a bottle opener. He said, "There. None of that's good for me."

After he picked up his crayons and pajamas and decided to leave his toothbrush, he slammed through the back door and said, "That'll teach her to call me hateful. I'll live in the tree, and then she won't have to bother loving me."

He ran to the tree. It was a huge tree with clumpy, lime green leaves and branches so heavy they reached almost to the ground. It was hollow at the bottom, and he was just the right size to fit in the opening. No one else can get in here, he thought, and then he laughed at the idea of his mother trying to crawl into the tree. He sat in there all afternoon. By the time the sun started to droop behind the house, he'd eaten all the cookies and the cake, most of the olives, and he'd even drunk the Coke. He had to admit his stomach felt like a sidewalk, all hard and stepped on. But he wouldn't leave the tree.

When it was really dark, not just the kind where there are shadows and you can really see things if you squint, but the kind where everything is black and you can't even see your skin, he heard his mother say, "George Henry, I know you're in that tree. Come in the house this minute."

"No, I live out here now. Just leave a plate on the back step like you do for Gregor, the cat." Inside the tree his words hit the bark and bounced back. An owl started screeching. He heard his mother's steps outside the tree.

"What's the matter, George Henry? Are you mad at me?"

He said, "You're mad at me, and you said I was hateful and not worth the bother."

His words echoed again. He didn't like the sound, and he was getting cramped inside the tree.

"I'm not angry," his mother said.

"You will be again someday, and then I'll just have to move out here again." He decided the floor was made of acorns. They kept bumping his legs.

She said, "Don't you know you get most angry with the people you love? Just because I get angry doesn't mean you're not worth the bother."

He nudged his head out the opening. "Honest?"

She said, "Sure, George Henry. We get angry with those we love most because we want them to be better than anyone else."

"But I'm not," he said.

She said, "I know it. But I love you anyhow."

He said, "I think I'll come out."

He did. As they shuffled toward the house, he said, "I hope tomorrow won't be one of those days."

It wasn't.

When Wendy Came

Craig Nagel

Robin was excited. She could hardly wait. She was so excited that she squirmed up and down in her desk and chewed little toothprints in her pencil.

Today was a very special day. At home all the furniture was dusted, the blue vase on the coffee table was filled with beautiful flowers, and outside the sidewalk was freshly swept. Today was a very special day. For today Mother was coming home from the hospital, and with her would come Wendy.

Robin had never seen her new baby sister in person, but she had seen a picture of her. Wendy didn't look very pretty in the picture because she was crying and her skin was all wrinkled up; her head looked far too big and her body far too small. But Daddy said she looked much better now, and Robin could hardly wait.

Finally the bell rang, and Miss Ran-

dell dismissed the class row by row. Robin ran as fast as she could all the way home. She was just turning the last corner before her house when she saw their blue station wagon drive up the driveway. Wendy was home!

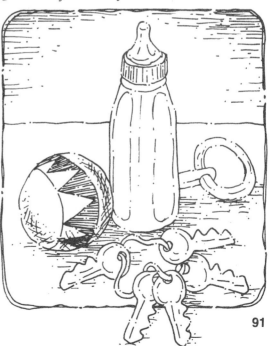

Robin burst into the living room all out of breath. There was Mother, sitting on the sofa, and in Mother's lap was a big puffy bundle of blankets and lace.

Robin peeked in between the pink blankets and the dainty white lace and saw a pair of big blue eyes looking at her. The eyes were so big and so blue that they looked exactly like glowing Christmas tree lights.

"Hi," said Robin. "How are you?"

"Waahh!" said Wendy. "Waahh!"

"She sure cries loud," said Robin, turning to her father. "Especially for her size."

"You're right," said her father. "But it seems to me that you cried just as loud when you were tiny."

Robin laughed and looked again at the big blue eyes that peered out of the blanket. She was glad that her new baby sister was home, but she wondered what it would be like if she always cried so loudly.

"Will Wendy always cry so loud?"

"No, darling," said Mother. "It's just that right now she has no other way of talking to us. She doesn't know any words, of course, and when she is hungry or wet, she wants to let us know about it. The only way she can do that is by crying."

Just then Wendy began to cry again, and her big blue eyes filled with sparkling tears.

"I think she might be hungry," said Mother.

"Waahh! Waahh! Waaaahhh!" cried Wendy, and the noise was so loud that Robin put her hands over her ears and wrinkled her nose. This baby was certainly going to be a nuisance. She looked at her father to see if he felt the same way. Her father was smiling, and so was her mother. Robin was puzzled. How could her parents be so happy when it was so noisy?

She was thinking about going back outside where it was quiet when Mother said, "Robin, would you please go into the kitchen and get Wendy's milk from the refrigerator? It's in a plastic bottle."

Robin marched into the kitchen with a frown on her face. Wendy this, Wendy that, she thought. All of a sudden everything is Wendy. What happened to me?

When she returned with the bottle, she handed it to Mother without saying a word. Then she turned and walked down the hallway to her room. She closed the door tight because Wendy was still crying, and she couldn't stand the noise.

She flopped down on her bed and cradled her head in her arms. What a sad thing, she thought. Here I was all excited about seeing Wendy, and now when I see her, all she does is make noise. I almost wish she had never been born.

Outside it was very quiet. Through the window at the side of her bed came the gentle sound of the afternoon breeze in the trees. Robin listened to the wind. She wished she could climb up into a tall tree and stay in the green leafy branches forever. At least it would be quiet up there.

She was trying to imagine how the world would look from the top of a giant tree when through the window came a faint peeping sound.

Robin crawled over to the window and looked out. On the branch of a middle-sized tree was a round brown nest, and in the nest were three baby robins.

"Peep," peeped one of the robins. Its mouth opened so wide that all Robin could see was a big hollow throat.

"Peep," went the second one.

"Peep, peep," went the third.

Just then a shadow passed over, and the next moment Robin saw the mother bird land on the edge of the nest. A long juicy worm dangled from the mother's beak, and in a moment the little birds stopped peeping and started to eat. When they were finished, the mother bird flew off in search of another worm, and the babies started to peep again.

Robin stretched back out on her bed and cradled her head in her arms. She thought about the baby birds and about the mother bird and about her baby sister, Wendy.

Then she jumped out of bed and walked into the living room. Wendy was still crying, but the noise didn't seem as loud.

Robin kneeled down on the rug in front of her baby sister and looked into her big blue eyes. "Welcome home," she said.

Friends Again

Susan Davis Sandberg

"No fooling around tonight, boys!" Glen heard Dad say as he left the room. Glen lay still in his top bunk. He was thinking about the picnic the next day—the first family picnic of the year.

He watched a spider slide down a white thread above him. He didn't see Rick sneak up and reach for his toe. But he felt him yank it.

"Hey, cut that out!" Glen yelled. He hung down over the edge of the bed to see if Rick was in the bunk below.

But Rick popped up near the end of the bed and tickled Glen's feet. Glen pulled his feet away so fast he fell to the floor with a loud thump. He was still there when Dad came in.

"Dad—" Glen started. Before he could finish, the sweep of Dad's big hand caught him smartly on the seat.

"No excuses!" Dad said angrily. "It was your voice I heard, and you are out of bed."

Glen rubbed the tears out of his eyes. He hurried into bed so Rick wouldn't see them. He bounced down hard as he pulled the covers up under his chin. He wished the spring would sink and hit Rick on the head.

He rubbed the sting and muttered, "It isn't fair. Not fair at all." No one heard him. Soon he fell asleep.

The buzz of Dad's razor woke him. Glen jumped down. His feet smacked the floor hard. The sound was clear and strong and angry.

He dragged his slippers as he walked past the bathroom.

"Hi, Glen," Dad called. Glen did not answer.

"Is that you, Glen?" Mother asked as he entered the kitchen. "Put these grapefruit halves on the table for me, will you?" She turned. "One's for you and one's for Dad."

"I don't want any!" Glen said, pouting.

Mother looked surprised. "Glen, you love grapefruit." Then she noticed his frown. "Whatever is the matter?" she asked.

Glen told her. Just as he finished, Dad came in with Rick.

Dad put his hand on Glen's shoulder as he said, "Rick told me about last night. I'm very sorry. Will you forgive me?"

Glen saw the sadness in his father's face, but he turned away. Then he jerked his shoulder from under his father's hand.

No one said anything as they sat down at the table. Everyone prayed together— everyone but Glen.

Dad buttered his toast slowly. He asked, "Why do we say, 'Forgive us our trespasses as we forgive those who trespass against us' when we pray?"

Rick piped up, "God wants you to forgive others like he forgives you."

Glen slumped in his chair, his face angry red.

Rick looked at Glen. "What's the matter with you anyway?" Rick said. "I forgave you last week when you broke my only bat."

Glen stared at the cereal in his bowl. He remembered how glad he was Rick didn't get mad at him.

Soon Dad pushed back his chair. He picked up the stack of towels. Rick grabbed the swimsuits. Glen stuffed his hands into his pockets.

Dad called back, "Glen, bring your ball and mitt. We'll give that pitching arm of yours a real workout today."

Glen thought for a minute. Then, pounding the ball into the mitt, Glen walked out to the car.

Dad saw his smile and asked, "Are we friends again?"

"We sure are!" Glen replied. He looked up at his tall father and wondered why he hadn't made up before this.

"Glad you're not mad anymore," Rick said.

Glen climbed in the car and punched his brother playfully. "Me too," he said, grinning.

Mean Herbie

Gloria A. Truitt

One afternoon while Johnny and his mother were in the bookstore, Johnny noticed a big, beautiful book about dogs. Quickly he took it from the shelf and began to turn the pages. "Oh, look, Mom!" Johnny said. "I've always wanted a book like this! Would you please buy it for me?"

Mother turned the book over to look at the price tag, then sadly shook her head. "I'm sorry, Johnny. I know you'd like to have this book, but I just can't afford it right now."

Although Johnny was disappointed, he understood, and without asking again, he put the book back on the shelf.

A week went by, then one afternoon Mother came into the house with a paper bag. "Johnny!" she called. "Come and see what I have for you!"

Quickly he took the bag and opened it. Inside the bag he found the beautiful dog book.

"I knew how much you wanted this book," said Mother, "and today I had some extra money."

"Oh, Mom! You're the greatest—thanks a million!" Johnny said as he began to turn the pages.

The next morning Johnny asked his mother if he could take his new book to school to show to his teacher and friends. "Of course you may," answered Mother, "but please take good care of it."

Mother was surprised to see Johnny crying when he came home for lunch. As he slumped down onto a kitchen chair, he said, "I'm so mad at Herbie, I could punch him in the nose!"

"Who's Herbie, and what happened?" asked Mother.

Johnny rubbed at his tears with the back of his hand. "Oh, he's a new kid in my class who's just plain mean! He grabbed my new book off my desk—and look what he did!"

Johnny pulled the book from beneath his jacket, and immediately his mother noticed the torn cover and wrinkled pages. "Now, Johnny, punching Herbie in the nose won't fix your book, but a little Scotch tape will. Let's see what we can do," suggested Mother.

Slowly and carefully, Mother repaired the book at the kitchen table while Johnny watched. He felt a little better because Mother was doing a good job of mending the rips and smoothing out the pages, but he was still very angry at Herbie.

"Why did Herbie tear your book, Johnny? Was it an accident?" asked Mother.

"No!" blurted Johnny. "He did it on purpose! Ever since he came to our school, he's been breaking things that belong to other kids. He's just jealous 'cause he doesn't have anything to bring to school."

"Well," said Mother, "have you ever tried sharing your things with Herbie so he wouldn't feel so left out? Maybe that's why he acts mean.''

"Hmmm, I guess I didn't share my book with him,'' muttered Johnny, "but do you really think that would have made any difference?''

"Why don't you think about it,'' suggested Mother.

After school the next day, Johnny came home very excited. "Guess what?'' he asked. "Our teacher is taking the whole class ice skating tomorrow at the new recreation center! Won't that be fun?''

"That's wonderful,'' said Mother.

Then Johnny explained that everyone was going except Herbie because he was the only one without ice skates.

"Someone said he could rent a pair at the center," said Johnny, "but Herbie said his family doesn't have money for renting skates. He looked terribly mean when he left school today!"

"I have an idea," said Mother. "What about the skates you've outgrown? If they fit, would you let Herbie borrow them?"

"I'm sure they'd fit him because he's smaller than I am," answered Johnny, "but I don't know if I should take them tomorrow. Knowing Herbie, he would probably wreck the skates!"

"I know you're still angry with Herbie because of the book, but why don't you take the skates anyway and see what happens," suggested Mother.

"Oh, all right," sighed Johnny, "but I *know* what's going to happen."

The next day, Mother waited for Johnny to come home from the skating party. She was curious to hear if Herbie had gone to the party with the rest of the class. At three o'clock Johnny ran into the house yelling, "Mother! Mother! Guess what? My old skates fit Herbie just right—and he didn't even break them! In fact, he took *good* care of them!"

"That's wonderful!" said Mother, "but where are they now?"

"Oh! I forgot to tell you," said Johnny as he opened the cookie jar for a snack. "Herbie and I decided to go skating together every Saturday, so I thought it would be much easier if I *gave* him the skates! You know, Mother, I don't know what was more fun—the skating party or giving my old skates to Herbie!"

Love Is a Helper

Ann Hudson Downs

A long line of cars, most of them driven by mothers, inched bumper to bumper into the pick-up lane. In the brief moment they were allowed to stop, children climbed inside.

Julie and Johnny's eyes became anxious when they saw their father in the driver's seat.

"Where's Mom?" they asked at the same time as they scrambled into the back seat.

"Your grandmother is sick and needs your mother to stay with her for a few days," their father told them.

The children suddenly became quiet.

"Your mother was sorry to leave without telling you good-bye, but she barely had time to catch the bus after the phone call," their father explained. "We'll make out just fine."

"I know," Julie said, almost in a whisper. "All the same, I wish Mom hadn't gone."

"But families should stick together and help each other," Dad told them. "Remember how glad we were to have Grandmother with us when Johnny was sick last summer?"

"I guess so," Johnny mumbled.

When Dad saw their sad faces in the rearview mirror, he tried to change the subject. "How would you like to go by the ice cream place?" he asked.

"I'm not hungry," Julie answered.

"Neither am I," Johnny agreed.

Nobody talked the rest of the way home. The children usually raced up the walk, glad to be home. But not today.

"When will Mom come home?" Julie asked as they entered the house.

"In a few days," Dad said. "In the meantime, I need help. We don't want her to come home and find everything in a mess."

"What can we do?" Julie asked.

"Right now, I'm hungry," Dad said. "Let's make some sandwiches for supper, and then we can make plans."

"I'll set the table," Julie announced.

"I'll put the napkins around and get the chairs ready," Johnny offered.

When supper was over, Dad washed and Julie wiped the dishes while Johnny fed Bozo, the dog. Then Johnny swept the kitchen and Julie emptied the wastebasket.

"Now let's plan," Julie said. She pulled a notebook from her book satchel and climbed up on the couch beside her father and Johnny. "I'll make a list the way Mom does so we won't forget."

"Let's see," Dad said. "The flowers will need water." Julie carefully printed *water flowers*.

They thought and thought. By bedtime they had a long list of things to be done by Julie and Johnny each afternoon when they came home from school. With so much to be done, they were too busy to be lonely. While Dad cut the grass and trimmed the shrubbery, Julie and Johnny did their work. Julie carefully checked the things they did off the list. Every night after supper they helped Dad put the kitchen in order, and Johnny always remembered to feed Bozo.

On Friday afternoon, as soon as Julie and Johnny were settled in the car, Dad told them the good news. "We'll have to hurry with our work today," he said, "so we can meet the six o'clock bus."

"Mom is coming home!" both children shouted at once.

When six o'clock came, Dad and the children were waiting, and sure enough, there was Mom. Everybody talked at once, but they saved the surprises.

The sign Julie and Johnny had made the night before was hanging on the door. It said, "We love you, Mom. Welcome home." Their mother was so pleased she gave everybody a big bear hug.

When they opened the door, their mother had the biggest surprise of all. "The house looks beautiful!" she cried.

"We'll keep on helping," Julie promised. "It was fun, and besides, it makes us feel good."

"Our children are growing up," Dad said. Then everybody laughed, just because it was so good to be together again.

Jerry's Train Ride

Ann L. Lamp

I 'm all ready, Mom!" Jerry Daniels called excitedly.

"All right, Jerry, I'll be downstairs in a minute," his mother answered.

This was going to be a very special afternoon. Jerry and his mother were going for a train ride! Jerry had never ridden on a train before, and he could hardly wait for his mother to get ready.

"We're on our way," Mother said. She smiled at Jerry as she put on her coat.

"Good!" he said. Jerry thought the time would never pass.

"We'll park the car at the depot and get on the train. Then we'll ride to the next town and back," Mother explained as she drove downtown.

"What is a *depot*?" Jerry asked. He'd never heard that word before.

"It's another name for the train station," his mother told him.

Once Jerry got aboard the train, he could hardly wait for it to start moving.

"Where are all these other people going?" Jerry asked.

"Some are probably going visiting, and some may be going to other cities on business. People travel for many different reasons, Jerry," Mother answered.

Several of the passengers smiled at Jerry. He smiled back and thought it great fun for them all to be riding the train together.

Just then the great long train gave a lurch!

"Mom! Mom! We're starting to move!" Jerry very nearly shouted as he felt the train begin to roll down the tracks.

Jerry watched as the depot and the other trains that were standing still passed out of sight. He watched out the window a long while. Pretty soon all the houses in the city had been left behind.

"Mom, look at all the black and white cows in that field," Jerry exclaimed.

Then Jerry was quiet for a while. It was fun to just sit back against the soft cushions and feel himself moving along with the train. He liked the gentle swaying motion.

He saw birds and a big pig with several baby pigs beside her. Jerry saw two tiny black cocker spaniel puppies playing near the railroad tracks. He hoped they were careful and didn't get too close.

Sometimes he saw people and cars. Even they looked different from the window of a moving train.

Jerry sat for a long time without saying anything. He was thinking very hard about something.

"Why are you so quiet, Jerry?" Mom asked.

"I was wondering something about God," Jerry explained.

"What about God?" Mother wanted to know.

"How does God know where we are? We're not at home now, and he won't know where to find us," Jerry said. "And what about these other people on our train? God won't know where they are either."

"Why, Jerry, God is looking down on us this very minute. He sees us wherever we are," Mother told him.

"But how does he know where we are this very minute?"

"He can see us because God can see everywhere. He is watching over us every minute of every single day," Mother said.

"How can he do that?"

"Well, Jerry, God is very different from you and me. He is in heaven and is able to see everything and everybody. He knows we're riding on a train and will see that we have a safe journey," his mother told him.

Jerry felt better. He sat back and enjoyed the rest of the train ride. He knew that God could see him riding on the train with his mother.

The Why Boy

James S. Kerr

Like almost every little boy who ever lived, Jimmy West was a "why" boy.

"Why does the sun come up at dawn? Where does it go when it sets? Why does the moon come up at night?"

Jimmy's mother usually knew the answers to his questions. If she didn't, then his father did. There were questions to ask about everything.

"Why is the grass green? Why do balls bounce? Why is my dog brown?"

There were so many things to do and see and ask questions about that Jimmy could not keep his mind on one thing for very long. He'd ask his mother a question, and just as soon as she answered, Jimmy would have another question to ask.

One bright Sunday afternoon, Jimmy's father suggested that the family go on a picnic. Jimmy liked to go on picnics.

It was fun to help pack the lunch and load up the car with all the good things. But most of all, Jimmy loved picnics because of the many new things he would see. And that meant a lot of new things to ask "why" about.

"Time to go," Father called.

Jimmy ran to get the basket. Jimmy sometimes forgot things—but not lunch!

Soon Jimmy and his father and mother were out of the city, driving along a country road.

"Watch for a good place for us to have our picnic," Mother said.

"OK," said Jimmy. He looked for a nice, grassy place for them to stop. Soon they came to a big, open field where the grass was long and green.

"There's a place," Jimmy said.

"No," Father said. "Not that one."

"Why?" asked Jimmy.

"The grass is too long, and there isn't any shade."

"Look again," Mother said.

Jimmy looked. Down the road they drove, until they came to a bridge that crossed a crooked little river.

"Look," said Mother. "There's a pretty little river running out to sea!"

"Why?" asked Jimmy.

"To help fill the big ocean."

"Why?" asked Jimmy.

And Father said:

"So there's a place for boats to sail,

"To make a playground for the whale,

"A place for winds to pick up rain,

"So everything will grow again."

They drove across the bridge and up the hill on the other side of the river. There were hills and trees and little valleys.

"I see a place," said Jimmy. He pointed to a spot not far from the road. There were large trees for shade and a

grassy spot to sit. There was even a place to park the car.

"It looks good to me," said Father.

"I like it too," Mother said.

Jimmy was glad they liked the place he had chosen. He helped carry the things from the car. Father carried the big lunch basket and put it under the tree.

"Can we eat now?" Jimmy asked.

"All right, Jimmy," Mother said. She opened the big basket and set plates for the three of them on the blanket.

"Jimmy," Father said. "Will you ask the blessing?"

"All right," Jimmy said. He folded his hands and prayed:

"Dear Jesus, thank you for this day,
"For watching o'er me when I play,
"Thank you for my health and food,
"And help me, Jesus, to be good.
"Amen."

Jimmy said the prayer so quickly that it really sounded more like a bumblebee than a little boy! He was so hungry that he began to eat the very second he said amen.

Father looked at Mother and Mother looked at Father. Then they both looked at Jimmy.

"Jimmy," Mother said, "you shouldn't mumble your prayers so fast."

"Why?" said Jimmy.

Father looked at Mother and Mother looked at Father. Then they both shook their heads.

Just then a big fat robin flew over to the tree. It sat on a branch right over Jimmy's head.

"See the big robin?" Mother asked.

"Yes," Jimmy said, "I see him."

Then the robin started to sing. It was a beautiful song.

"Why is he singing?" Jimmy asked.

"He's thanking God for this sunny day," said Father.

"Oh," said Jimmy.

The robin stopped singing and flew over to the fence. Then a red and white spotted calf came over to the fence.

"Moo-oo," said the calf.

"Why is he moo-oo-ing?" Jimmy asked.

"He's thanking God for the green grass," said Father.

Jimmy looked over to the field again and saw a chicken scratching on the ground.

"Cluck, cluck," said the chicken.

"Why is the chicken clucking?" asked Jimmy.

"She's thanking God for the fat kernels of grain," said Mother.

After a while, Jimmy looked up at his mother and said, "Can God understand the robin's song?"

"Yes," said Mother.

"Can God understand the calf too?"

"Yes," said Father.

"Can God understand the chicken?"

"Yes," said Mother.

"They all have a happy song for God," Father said, "thanking him for all good things."

All at once Jimmy knew why his mother and father had looked at him when he prayed so fast.

"I guess I just mumbled words," Jimmy said.

Mother smiled. And Father smiled.

"But when I pray, I'm talking to God!" said Jimmy.

"That's right," said Mother. "And when you talk so fast, and sound like a bumblebee instead of a thankful little boy, you're only thinking of eating."

"But God wants to hear me too, doesn't he?" asked Jimmy. "Just like he hears the birds and calves and chickens?"

"Yes," Mother said.

"From now on I'm going to talk to God more often in my language. I'll take my time so he'll know I'm thankful too!" said Jimmy.

"In what language will you talk to God?" asked Father.

"Prayer!" said Jimmy.

Mother smiled and Father smiled, because this time Jimmy didn't have to ask "why" or "how" or "what." He already knew the answer!

I Am Glad

Ruth Cox Anderson

*I have feet and I can run,
when I play I have such fun.
I have hands and I can do
most anything that I want to.
I have eyes and I can see*

*all the things God planned for me.
I have ears and I can hear
sounds that come from far and near.
I have a voice and I can pray
to thank God for each lovely day.*

Prayers

Jesus, Tender Shepherd, Hear Me

Mary L. Duncan

Jesus, tender Shepherd, hear me,
bless thy little lamb tonight;
through the darkness be thou near me,
keep me safe till morning light.

Through this day thy hand has led me,
and I thank thee for thy care;
thou hast warmed me, clothed and fed me,
listen to my evening prayer.

A Children's Prayer

Gloria A. Truitt

God, thank you for my daily bread,
my pillow, and my snuggly bed.
God, thank you for my mom and dad
who love me when I'm good—or bad.
God, thank you for the winter snow,
the summer rain that makes plants grow.
But most of all, I thank you for
just being with me—evermore.

Dear Father, Hear and Bless

Author unknown

Dear Father, hear and bless
thy beasts and singing birds.
And guard with tenderness
small things that have no words.

Both Strong and Gentle

Lois Walfrid Johnson

How strong you are, God,
as strong as an ocean wave
dancing against tall rocks.
Yet how gentle you are too,
as gentle
as pale moonlight
softening the darkness.
Thank you for being
both strong and gentle,
both mighty and kind.

Moon and Stars

Ron and Lyn Klug

At night when it's dark
I can look out my window
and see the moon that glows
and the stars that twinkle.
Thank you for making them, God.

We're Thankful, Lord

Ron and Lyn Klug

When we're tired, Lord,
we're thankful for cozy beds
and warm blankets,
for good-night hugs and kisses.
Thank you for being with us
while we sleep.

People Who Take Care of Me

Lois Walfrid Johnson

Father in heaven,
be with all the people
who take care of me—
my mommy and daddy,
my brothers and sisters,
my grandma and grandpa,
my aunts and uncles and cousins,
and my baby-sitters.
I'm glad they love me.

The Moon and Planet Earth

Chris Jones

Great God, I'm glad you made the earth
the way you did.
The moon is empty with only rocks and dust,
but we have rivers, trees, and prairies,
deserts, canyons, flowers, and green grass.
The astronauts in their capsules say
the earth is full of color, the moon is not.
And so, O God,
for the beautiful planet Earth
you made for us,
I praise you.

Thank You, God

Lois Walfrid Johnson

Thank you
for my soft animals
and warm blankets.
Thank you
for hands that tuck me
into bed at night.
Thank you for watching over me
while I sleep.
Good-night, God.

At Day's End

Lois Walfrid Johnson

God, bless the good things
I did today—
the picture I colored,
the dandelions I picked,
the table I set for Mommy.
Thanks for being with me.

People Who Work at Night

Ron and Lyn Klug

Father in heaven,
be with all the people who work at night:
policemen and firemen who protect us,
doctors and nurses who help sick people,
all those who make the things we need.
While they work, I am sleeping.
Be with me too, Lord.

My Family

Lois Walfrid Johnson

Thanks for giving me
to Mommy and Daddy,
and thanks for giving
Mommy and Daddy to me.
I'm glad you made us a family.

Nights Are for Resting

Ron and Lyn Klug

This has been a busy day, Lord.
Now my body needs rest.
Help me have a good sleep
so I'll be able to play tomorrow.
Please be with me through the night.

The Dark Is Friendly

Chris Jones

Thank you for making the night, God.
It's fun to play out in the dark,
to run and hide or just kick a ball.
The dark is friendly,
and I like to look at the stars.
Thank you for nighttime, God,
for fun in the dark
and for time to sleep.

Thunder and Lightning

Lois Walfrid Johnson

Sometimes the thunder
sounds like people
clapping their hands.
Thank you, God,
that you're strong enough
to make the lightning flash
and the wind blow,
and that you're strong enough
to take care of me.

Messed Up Days

Chris Jones

I'm sorry, Lord. It's been a bad day.
I've messed up so many things today.
Please wash away
all the wrong things I've said
and done and thought.
Thank you for your promise in the Bible
to forgive
because I know you will forgive me too.
So please hear me and help me
to make tomorrow a better day.

Lullabies

God My Father, Loving Me

G. W. Briggs   J. Knecht

Key of G

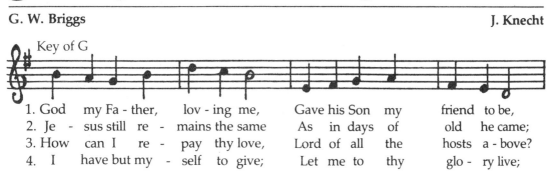

1. God my Fa - ther, lov - ing me, Gave his Son my friend to be,
2. Je - sus still re - mains the same As in days of old he came;
3. How can I re - pay thy love, Lord of all the hosts a - bove?
4. I have but my - self to give; Let me to thy glo - ry live;

Gave his Son my form to take, Bear - ing all things for my sake.
As my broth - er by my side, Still he seeks my steps to guide.
What have I, a child, to bring Un - to thee, thou heav'n - ly King?
Let me fol - low, day by day, Where thou show - est me the way.

The Quiet Nighttime

M. Elizabeth Suiter   Philip R. Dietterich

Key of A minor

1. I like the qui - et night - time, When God is with me still:__
2. I like the qui - et night - time, When I'm all tucked in bed:__
3. I like the qui - et night - time, When crick-ets sing to me:__

I go out-side and look up high And watch the bright stars in the sky.
I peek out at the big soft night And see my neigh - bor's friend-ly light.
I think of God's kind friend-ly ways, Of his good plans for nights and days.

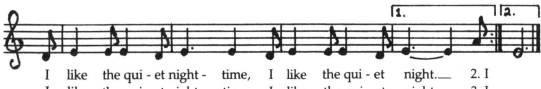

I like the qui - et night - time, I like the qui - et night.__ 2. I
I like the qui - et night - time, I like the qui - et night.__ 3. I
I like the qui - et night - time, I like the qui - et night.

He's Got the Whole World in His Hands

Spiritual

Key of F

1. He's got the whole world— in his hands,— He's got the whole world— in his hands,— He's got the whole world— in his hands,— He's got the whole world in his hands.

2. He's got the wind and rain in his hands.
3. He's got that little baby in his hands.
4. He's got you and me in his hands.
5. He's got everybody in his hands.
6. He's got the whole world in his hands.

Hush, Little Baby

Traditional American

Key of F

1. Hush, lit - tle ba - by, don't say a word, Dad-dy's gon-na buy you a mock - ing bird, And if that mock - ing bird won't sing, Dad-dy's gon-na buy you a dia - mond ring. 2. (And)

2. And if that diamond ring turns to brass,
   Daddy's gonna buy you a looking glass,
   And if that looking glass gets broke,
   Daddy's gonna buy you a billy goat.

3. And if that billy goat won't pull,
   Daddy's gonna buy you a cart and bull,
   And if that cart and bull turn over,
   Daddy's gonna buy you a dog named Rover.

4. And if that dog named Rover won't bark,
   Daddy's gonna buy you a horse and cart,
   And if that horse and cart fall down,
   You'll still be the sweetest little baby in town.

Kumbaya

Key of D

1. Kum - ba - ya, my Lord, kum - ba - ya,

Kum - ba - ya, my Lord, kum - ba - ya.

Kum - ba - ya, my Lord, kum - ba - ya,—

Oh, Lord— kum - ba - ya.

2. Someone's sleeping, Lord, kumbaya, (three times)
   Oh, Lord, kumbaya.

   (repeat verse one after each verse)

3. Someone's crying, Lord, kumbaya, (three times)
   Oh, Lord, kumbaya.

4. Someone's praying, Lord, kumbaya, (three times)
   Oh, Lord, kumbaya.

5. Someone's shouting, Lord, kumbaya, (three times)
   Oh, Lord, kumbaya.

6. Someone's singing, Lord, kumbaya, (three times)
   Oh, Lord, kumbaya.

7. Someone's worshiping, Lord, kumbaya, (three times)
   Oh, Lord, kumbaya.

All Praise to Thee, My God, This Night

Thomas Kent
Thomas Tallis

Key of G

1. All praise to thee, my God, this night For all the bless-ings of the light.
2. For-give me, Lord, for thy dear Son, The ill that I this day have done;
3. Teach me to live, that I may dread The grave as lit-tle as my bed.
4. Oh, may my soul in thee re-pose, And may sweet sleep mine eye-lids close,
5. Praise God, from whom all bless-ings flow; Praise him all crea-tures here be-low;

Keep me, oh, keep me, King of kings, Be-neath thine own al-might-y wings.
That with the world, my-self, and thee, I, ere I sleep, at peace may be.
Teach me to die, that so I may Rise glo-rious at the awe-some day.
Sleep that shall me more vig-'rous make To serve my God when I a-wake!
Praise him a-bove, ye heav'n-ly host; Praise Fa-ther, Son, and Ho-ly Ghost.

Father, We Thank Thee for the Night

Rebecca J. Weston

Daniel Batchellor

Key of G

1. Fa-ther, we thank thee for the night, And for the pleas-ant morn - ing light;
2. Help us to do the things we should, To be to oth - ers kind and good;

For rest and food and lov - ing care, And all that makes the day so fair.
In all we do in work or play, To grow more lov-ing ev - 'ry day.

Who Made the Stars

Miriam Drury

Miriam Drury

Key of D

1. Who made the stars in the wide blue sky? God our Fa - ther.
2. Who made the flowers and trees to grow?
3. Who made the peo - ple ev' - ry-where?

Who made the bees and birds that fly? God our lov - ing Fa - ther.
Who made the rain - drops and the snow?
Who gives to all his love and care?

Jesus Loves Me When I'm Sad

Sylvia Gentz

Robert J. Powell

Key of D

1. Je - sus loves me when I'm sad, Je - sus loves me when I'm glad,
2. Je - sus loves me when it's night, Je - sus loves me when it's light,

When I'm sick or when I play, Je - sus loves me ev - 'ry - day.
When I sing, and when I play, Je - sus loves me ev - 'ry - day.

Jesus Loves Me, Jesus Loves Me

Traditional Swedish

Key of F

1. Je - sus loves me, Je - sus loves me, He is al - ways, al - ways near.
2. Je - sus loves me, night and morn - ing, Je - sus hears the prayers I pray.

If I al - ways trust and love him There is noth-ing I need fear.
And he nev - er, nev-er leaves me When I work or when I play.

Je-sus loves me, Je - sus loves me, He is al - ways, al - ways near.
Je - sus loves me, night and morn - ing, Je-sus hears the prayers I pray.

All Through the Night

Traditional English

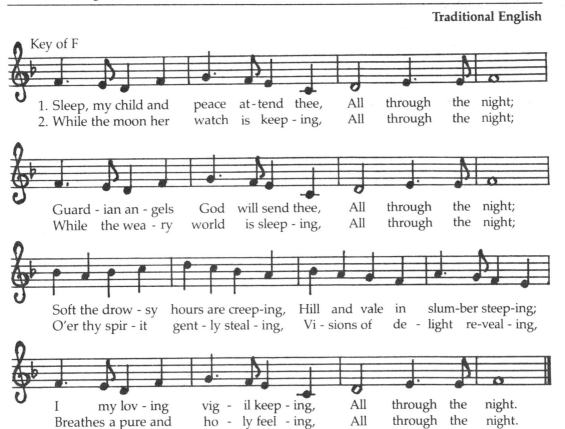

Key of F

1. Sleep, my child and peace at-tend thee, All through the night;
2. While the moon her watch is keep-ing, All through the night;

Guard - ian an - gels God will send thee, All through the night;
While the wea - ry world is sleep - ing, All through the night;

Soft the drow - sy hours are creep-ing, Hill and vale in slum-ber steep-ing;
O'er thy spir - it gent - ly steal - ing, Vi - sions of de - light re-veal - ing,

I my lov - ing vig - il keep-ing, All through the night.
Breathes a pure and ho - ly feel - ing, All through the night.

We Thank Thee, Lord

V. T. Nye

German Round

① Key of G

1. For all thy lov - ing care, We thank thee, Lord.
2. For all thy lov - ing care, We thank thee, Lord.

②

Thanks for the food we eat, And for the friends we meet.
Keep - ing us by thy side, Ev - er to be our guide.

③

For each new day we greet, We thank thee, Lord.
For all that you pro - vide, We thank thee, Lord.

ACKNOWLEDGMENTS

We would like to acknowledge the following sources of the stories, poems, prayers, and lullabies appearing in this collection.

"Lullaby Story" and "Everything, Praise the Lord!" by Carol Greene, "When God Made the World" and "Carlos Sees God's Fireworks" by Elizabeth Friedrich, "Michael's Mitten" by Donna Bobb, and "Tassy, Come Home" by Sue Richterkessing originally appeared in *Happy Times*, © Concordia Publishing House, and are used by permission.

"Sid's Spooky Closet" by Eileen Cole, "Kitten Fight" by Catharine Brandt, "The Circus Balloon" by Penny Jans, "Jenny's Droopy Tulip" by Martha P. Johnson, "A Problem for Robby" and "Stolen Treasure" by Lois Kaufmann, "The Boy Who Loved the Wind" by Betty Lou Mell, "Mr. Grumble and the Missing Smile," "Mean Herbie," and "A Children's Prayer" by Gloria A. Truitt, and "Love One Another" by Helen Kronberg originally appeared in *Story Friends*, © Mennonite Publishing House, and are used by permission.

"Michael's Problem" by Betty M. Hockett, "Teddy's Friend" by Mildred Sallee, "The Birthday Party" by Helen Kronberg, "Friday Helpers" and "Joey's Surprise" by Ann Hudson Downs, "The Scary Scritch" by Peg Roberts, "Billy's Promise" by Kit Lambeth, and "Night Sounds" by Betty Brown originally appeared in *Wonder Time*, © Department of Children's Ministries, Church of the Nazarene, and are used by permission.

"Bedtime Wishes" by M. Ogden and "Shadows" by Esther A. Middlewood originally appeared in *Listen*, © Department of Children's Ministries, Church of the Nazarene, and are used by permission.

"Every Dog Should Have a Boy" by Betty Lou Mell originally appeared in *Discoveries*, © Department of Children's Ministries, Church of the Nazarene, and are used by permission.

"A Good Feeling" by Verna Sherman originally appeared in *Read and Do*, © Gospel Publishing House, and is used by permission.

"Anything—Even Socks" by Joyce Ellis originally appeared in a collection of short stories by Joyce Ellis entitled *Wee Pause*. Copyright 1977 by Bible Memory Association of St. Louis. Used by permission.

"I Am Glad" by Ruth Cox Anderson is reprinted from *Nursery Days*, March 13, 1977. Copyright © 1977 by Graded Press.

"Roller Skates" by Mae M. Vanderboom, "Grandmother's Little Game" by Claire Lynn, "When Will the Sun Shine?" by Sharon Ihnen, "What's the Difference?" by Lois Holm, "Move Along," "The Boy Who Liked God," and "One of Those Days" by Ron Matthies, "The Broken Window" by Elizabeth Wedge, "David and the Jellyfish" by Sue Guist, "A Nickel Bet," "Autumn Sigh," and "When Wendy Came" by Craig Nagel, "Friends Again" by Susan Davis Sandberg, "Jerry's Train Ride" by Ann L. Lamp, "The Why Boy" by James S. Kerr, and "Good-Night, Dear World" by Solveig Paulson Russell originally appeared in *Hand in Hand*, copyright © Augsburg Publishing House.

"Both Strong and Gentle" is from *Just a Minute, Lord* by Lois Walfrid Johnson, copyright © 1973 Augsburg Publishing House.

"People Who Take Care of Me," "Thank You, God," "At Day's End," "My Family," and "Thunder and Lightning" are from *Hello, God* by Lois Walfrid Johnson, copyright © 1975 Augsburg Publishing House.

"The Moon and Planet Earth," "The Dark Is Friendly," and "Messed Up Days" are from *Lord, I Want to Tell You Something* by Chris Jones, copyright © 1973 Augsburg Publishing House.

"Moon and Stars" and "We're Thankful, Lord" are from *Thank You, God* by Ron and Lyn Klug, copyright © 1980 Augsburg Publishing House.

"People Who Work at Night" and "Nights Are for Resting" are from *Please, God* by Ron and Lyn Klug, copyright © 1980 Augsburg Publishing House.

"Jesus Loves Me When I'm Sad" is from *Young Children Sing* © 1967 Lutheran Church Press and Augsburg Publishing House.

"Who Made the Stars" words and music copyright, 1935, by the Presbyterian Board of Christian Education; renewed, 1963; from *When the Little Child Wants to Sing*. Used by permission of the Westminster Press, Philadelphia, Pa.

"The Quiet Nighttime" copyright 1966 by Graded Press. From *Sing and Be Joyful*. Used by permission.

"We Thank Thee, Lord" is from *Singing with Children* by Robert and Vernice Nye, Neva Aubin, and George Kyme. © 1962 by Wadsworth Publishing Co., Inc. Reprinted by permission of Wadsworth Publishing Co., Belmont, California 94002.